INTRODUCTION TO
MICROPROCESSOR
SYSTEM DESIGN

McGRAW-HILL SERIES IN ELECTRICAL ENGINEERING

Stephen W. Director, Carnegie-Mellon University
Consulting Editor

NETWORKS AND SYSTEMS

COMMUNICATIONS AND INFORMATION THEORY

CONTROL THEORY

ELECTRONICS AND ELECTRONIC CIRCUITS

POWER AND ENERGY

ELECTROMAGNETICS

COMPUTER ENGINEERING AND SWITCHING THEORY

INTRODUCTORY AND SURVEY

RADIO, TELEVISION, RADAR, AND ANTENNAS

Previous Consulting Editors

Computer Engineering
And Switching Theory

Stephen W. Director, Carnegie-Mellon University
Consulting Editor

HARRY GARLAND
President of Cromemco Incorporated
Lecturer in Electrical Engineering
Stanford University

INTRODUCTION TO
MICROPROCESSOR
SYSTEM DESIGN

McGRAW-HILL BOOK COMPANY
New York   St. Louis   San Francisco   Auckland   Bogotá   Düsseldorf
Johannesburg   London   Madrid   Mexico   Montreal   New Delhi
Panama   Paris   São Paulo   Singapore   Sydney   Tokyo   Toronto

Library of Congress Cataloging in Publication Data

Garland, Harry.
Introduction to microprocessor system design.

Includes bibliographical references and index.
1. Microprocessors.   I.   Title.
QA76.5.G327   001.6′4   78-11114
ISBN 0-07-022871-X
ISBN 0-07-022870-1 (pbk.)

INTRODUCTION TO MICROPROCESSOR
SYSTEM DESIGN

1 2 3 4 5 6 7 8 9 0   DO DO   7 8 3 2 1 0 9

This book was set in Helvetica Light by Black Dot, Inc.
The editors were Charles E. Stewart and
J. W. Maisel; the designer was Elliot Epstein;
the production supervisor was Dominick Petrellese.
The drawings were done by J & R Services, Inc.
R. R. Donnelley & Sons Company
was printer and binder.

CONTENTS

PREFACE

The microprocessor is a circuit component that has brought about a major change in the way electronic systems are designed. Microprocessors are used in applications as diverse as pocket calculators, laboratory instruments, consumer products, aircraft flight-control systems, and business computer systems. In each of these, and in many other applications, the microprocessor has made a major impact on the system design.

In this book, we examine the essence of the microprocessor, as well as how it works and how it can be used in system design. Emphasis is on the understanding and practical implementation of microprocessor-based designs. Specific design examples are used to illustrate the basic concepts.

Effective application of microprocessors requires a knowledge of both microprocessor *hardware* and microprocessor *software*. Both subjects are discussed in this book and each assumes some previous background of the reader. Background to the hardware chapters is assumed to be a one-year undergraduate electronics course or equivalent training. Basic transistor circuits, logic gates, and power-supply circuits should be familiar topics. Background to the software chapters is assumed to be an introduction to computer programming, a familiarity with the concept of a stored program, and a knowledge of the binary number system.

Chapter 1 describes what a microprocessor is and how it is used. Chapter 2 describes the integrated circuit technologies used in the construction of microprocessors. Several of the most popular microprocessors are introduced in Chap. 3, including the latest "single-chip" computers and powerful 16-bit processors. Chapter 4 describes the detailed circuitry required to use a microprocessor, and more advanced hardware concepts—interrupts, serial interfaces, and DMA—are deferred to Chap. 5.

Once the hardware of a microprocessor system is defined, the operation of the system is determined strictly by the system software. An introduction to microprocessor software is given in Chap. 6, followed by an introduction to higher level languages in Chap. 7.

The use of microprocessors to carry out arithmetic operations is described in Chap. 8. Techniques for using analog signals with digital microprocessors is discussed in Chap. 9. Finally, interface standards that can be used to greatly expand a microprocessor system are presented in Chap. 10.

This text is designed to be used in conjunction with the detailed manufacturers' literature available for specific microprocessors.

Harry Garland

INTRODUCTION TO
MICROPROCESSOR SYSTEM DESIGN

INTRODUCTION

Although many different types of microprocessors are available today, they share many features in common. In fact, as microprocessor designs have evolved over the last several years they have approached more and more closely the ideal of a self-contained "single-chip computer." Such a computer is fabricated as an integrated circuit (IC) on a single chip of silicon. It is able to execute stored programs and is designed to interface easily to external devices.

In this chapter the concept of an ideal microprocessor is introduced. Certain definitions and conventions used in discussing microprocessors are introduced and a generalized model is derived from the concept of the ideal microprocessor. With this generalized model in mind, you will be prepared to understand the operation of specific microprocessors as they are introduced in subsequent chapters.

THE IDEAL MICROPROCESSOR

Let's consider what might be called an "ideal" microprocessor. As shown in Fig. 1-1, the ideal microprocessor has N input lines and M output lines. Since the microprocessor is a digital device, only two permissible voltage levels may be applied to any input line. Similarly, only two possible output voltage levels can emerge at any output line. These two voltages are called *logic zero* and *logic one* and are symbolically represented by the binary digits (called *bits*) 0 and 1.

Signals on the input lines are the data input to the microprocessor. These data may come from switches, sensors, analog-to-digital converters, keyboards, or any number of other such devices. Inside this ideal microprocessor resides the microprocessor *program*. The program is a set of sequential instructions that determine how the input data is to be processed, and what information is to be sent to the output lines as a consequence

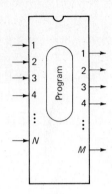

FIGURE 1–1
The ideal microprocessor.

of this input data. The output lines may be connected to actuators, digital displays, digital-to-analog converters, printers, alarms, or any of a variety of output devices.

Conceptually, then, a microprocessor is a digital device that accepts data from any number of input lines, processes the data according to the dictates of a stored program, and produces any number of output signals as a consequence of this data processing. At any given time, the logic levels on the output lines of a microprocessor are determined by just two factors:

1. The complete history of input signals to the microprocessor up to that time

2. The stored program of the microprocessor

The key to the great versatility of the microprocessor is that for the same or very similar hardware, programs can be designed for a great number of different applications.

For a specific example of where microprocessors are used, consider the control of traffic lights at an intersection. Each input line of the microprocessor is connected to a different sensor in the road. When an automobile passes over a sensor, a logic 1 appears on the corresponding input line; otherwise, the input line is at logic 0. Each output of the microprocessor controls a different lamp in the traffic light at the intersection. A logic 1 turns the lamp on, and a logic 0 turns it off. The program of the microprocessor is designed to expedite the safe flow of traffic at the intersection. Other inputs to the microprocessor could be used to indicate the time of day or, perhaps, the nature of the road conditions. Outputs from a microprocessor at one intersection might be used as inputs to a microprocessor at another intersection. With a sufficiently sophisticated microprocessor program, all these factors could be taken into account in the control of the traffic lights.

THE DATA BUS

Unlike the ideal microprocessor, real microprocessors cannot afford the luxury of N input lines and M output lines if the numbers N and M are very large. There are a limited number of pins available on any practical IC package. For most microprocessors, N is equal to M. This number is defined as the *data path width* or *word size* of the microprocessor. The single most common parameter used in microprocessor taxonomy is the data path width. The lines used to carry data to and from the microprocessor are collectively called the *data bus*.*

Figure 1-2*a* shows an 8-bit microprocessor which has an 8-bit-wide data path (that is, $N = M = 8$). This microprocessor operates on just 8 bits of data at any one time. A data word of 8 bits is defined as a *byte*. A compact notation for representing the 8-bit-wide data bus is shown in Fig. 1-2*b*. A 4-bit microprocessor is illustrated in Fig. 1-3. A 4-bit data word is defined as a *nybble*.

FIGURE 1-2
The 8-bit microprocessor. Each data word contains 8 bits or 1 byte.

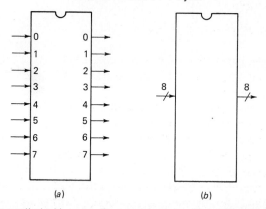

(a)   (b)

*Note that "bus" is spelled with *one s*. The word is derived from the Latin *omnibus* meaning "for all." Spelling confusion of this word in the electronics discipline most likely stems from the trademark Buss used to identify fuses manufactured by the Bussman Corporation.

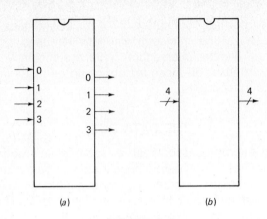

FIGURE 1–3
The 4-bit microprocessor. Each data word
contains 4 bits or 1 nybble.

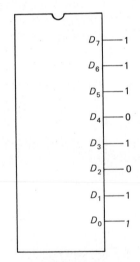

FIGURE 1–4
An 8-bit microprocessor data bus.
D7 is the most-significant bit
(MSB) and D0 is the least-
significant bit (LSB).

At any given time, the logic levels on the data lines of a microprocessor
define a specific data word. For the case of the 8-bit microprocessor shown
in Fig. 1-4, the data word is made up of the eight binary digits D0 through

TABLE 1-1
The Octal Digits

Binary number	Octal digit
000	0
001	1
010	2
011	3
100	4
101	5
110	6
111	7

D7. D0 is called the *least-significant bit* or LSB. D7 is called the *most-significant bit* or MSB. The data word on the data bus can be numerically represented in several different ways. The simplest way is in binary notation as a *binary number*. In this notation, the 8-bit data word shown in Fig. 1-4 is written as 11101011. To show that this is a binary number it can be suffixed by the letter B or the subscript 2 as shown:

$$11101011B \quad \text{or} \quad 11101011_2$$

This data word could also be represented as an *octal number*. In octal notation, each group of three binary digits is assigned a single number between zero and seven according to Table 1-1. This table can be used to find the octal equivalent for the binary word:

11	101	011	binary
3	5	3	octal

353 is the octal equivalent of the binary number 11101011. To show that the number is in octal notation it can be suffixed with the letter Q or the subscript 8 as shown:

$$353Q \quad \text{or} \quad 353_8$$

A third way to represent the data word (and the way most commonly used with microprocessors) is as a *hexadecimal number*. In hexadecimal notation, each group of 4 bits is assigned a single character according to Table 1-2. The hexadecimal equivalent for the binary number above can be found as follows:

TABLE 1-2
The Hexadecimal Digits

Binary number	Hexadecimal digit
0000	0
0001	1
0010	2
0011	3
0100	4
0101	5
0110	6
0111	7
1000	8
1001	9
1010	A
1011	B
1100	C
1101	D
1110	E
1111	F

1110 1011	binary
E B	hexadecimal

EB is the hexadecimal equivalent of the binary number 1110 1011 and the octal number 353. The word "hexadecimal" is commonly abbreviated simply as *hex*. A hex number can be suffixed with the letter H or the subscript 16 to show that it is written in hexadecimal notation:

$$\text{EBH} \quad \text{or} \quad \text{EB}_{16}$$

One of the most severe practical limitations of microprocessors is the limited number of pins available in an economical IC package. To save on the number of pins required, many microprocessors use the same pins for both the input data bus and the output data bus. At any given time, the pins are used either for input or output but are never used for both simultaneous-

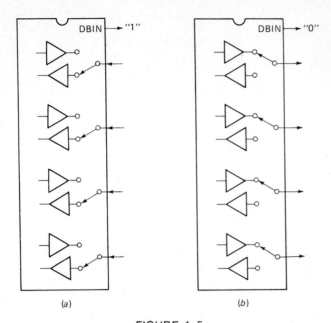

FIGURE 1-5
A 4-bit microprocessor showing the operation of the
bidirectional data bus. (*a*) Data bus in the input mode.
(*b*) Data bus in the output mode.

ly. Fig. 1-5 diagramatically shows a 4-bit microprocessor with a *bidirectional data bus*. Fig. 1-5*a* shows the data bus in the input mode and Fig. 1-5*b* shows the bus in the output mode.

Fig. 1-5 also shows a special *control output* of the microprocessor, DBIN in this case, that is used to indicate to external circuitry whether the data bus is in the input mode or the output mode. DBIN goes high (logic 1) to indicate the input mode and goes low (logic 0) to indicate the output mode.

The notation for representing the bidirectional data bus of an *N*-bit microprocessor is shown in Fig. 1-6.

THE ADDRESS BUS

For the ideal microprocessor, the output data can be a function of the total history of the input data. The nature of this function is determined by the microprocessor program. While the ideal microprocessor is assumed to have an unlimited internal memory, real microprocessors are necessarily limited in the amount of internal memory available for data and program storage. As a result, the microprocessor very often must have access to an

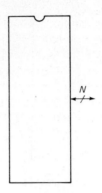

FIGURE 1–6
An N-bit microprocessor with a
bidirectional data bus.

external memory. In general, the microprocessor must be able to both store information in this memory and retrieve information from it. The process of storing information in memory is called *memory writing*. The process of retrieving information from memory is called *memory reading*.

Information is stored in memory at a set of memory locations. Each memory location contains one word of memory. The size of the memory word is determined by the data path width of the microprocessor. An 8-bit microprocessor, for example, requires each memory location to contain an 8-bit data word or byte. A different memory organization would be used for a 4-bit microprocessor, however, so that each memory location contained a 4-bit word or nybble.

Each location in memory has a unique *memory address*. Unless otherwise stated, this address will be specified using hexadecimal notation.

FIGURE 1–7
The address bus is used to select
memory locations in external
memory

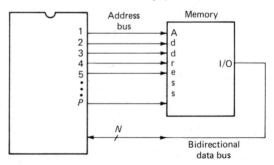

Before reading or writing at a memory location, the microprocessor must first select the desired memory address. Some microprocessors output this information on the data bus just prior to any memory read or write operation. Most microprocessors, however, have a separate *address bus* as shown in Fig. 1-7. Each line of the address bus can be either at logic 1 or at logic 0. Since each line has just two states, a microprocessor with P address lines is able to address 2^P unique memory locations. Table 1-3 shows the evaluation of 2^P for values of P ranging from 0 to 20.

TABLE 1-3
The Powers of 2

P	2^P
0	1
1	2
2	4
3	8
4	16
5	32
6	64
7	128
8	256
9	512
10	1024
11	2048
12	4096
13	8192
14	16384
15	32768
16	65536
17	131072
18	262144
19	524288
20	1048576

Example

The Z80 is an 8-bit microprocessor with 16 address lines. How many bytes of memory can the Z80 directly address?

Answer 2^{16} = 65,536 bytes.

The address word of a microprocessor is represented in hexadecimal notation in very much the same way as the data word. Take, for example, the microprocessor of Fig. 1-8 which has a 16-bit address bus with address lines labeled A0 through A15. In this example, the binary address on this address bus is 1110001111111111. Table 1-2 can be used to find the hexadecimal equivalent of this number:

$$
\begin{array}{ccccc}
1110 & 0011 & 1111 & 1111 & \text{binary} \\
\text{E} & 3 & \text{F} & \text{F} & \text{hex}
\end{array}
$$

The hexadecimal number E3FF is much more compact than its binary equivalent, and it is for this reason that hexadecimal notation is used.

The entire set of memory locations a microprocessor is able to access is called the *memory space*. Hexadecimal notation is used to represent the address of each location in memory space. For a microprocessor with a 16-bit address bus, the lowest memory location is at address 0000 while

FIGURE 1–8
A 16-bit address bus.

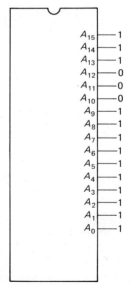

the highest memory location is at address FFFF, as illustrated in Fig. 1-9.

The size of the memory space is expressed in units of *kilowords*, where one kiloword equals 2^{10} or 1024 words. For the case of an 8-bit word the unit is a *kilobyte* which equals 1024 bytes. Although the prefix "kilo" usually refers to 1000 units, this somewhat unconventional usage is widespread in microprocessor nomenclature. Thus, an 8-bit microprocessor with a 16-bit address bus can address 64 kilobytes, or 64K of memory space.

When dealing with a 16-bit memory address, note that the most significant hexadecimal digit of the address denotes 4K boundaries of memory space, as shown in Fig. 1-10. The first 4K of memory, for example, runs from address 0000 to 0FFF; the next 4K from address 1000 to 1FFF; the next 4K from 2000 to 2FFF, and so on.

The 1K boundaries of memory are illustrated in Fig. 1-11. Note that there are 400H words of memory in each 1K of memory space. The addresses of the first 1K of memory range from 0000 to 03FF; the next 1K from 0400 to 07FF; the next 1K from 0800 to 0BFF; and the next 1K from 0C00 to 0FFF. The next 4K of memory, therefore, starts at address 1000.

In microprocessor work, 256 words of memory are called a *page* of memory. Each page of memory has 100H words. The addresses of the lowest page in memory range from 0000 to 00FF; the next page from 0100 to 01FF; and so on.

FIGURE 1–9
Memory space for a microprocessor with a 16-bit address bus can be visualized as a memory map of 65,536 addresses. The lowest address is 000H; the highest address is FFFFH.

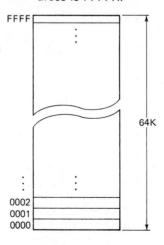

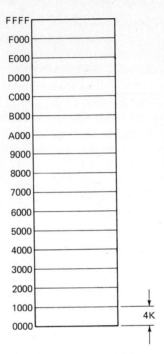

FIGURE 1–10
The most-significant digit of the
hexadecimal memory address in-
crements on 4K boundaries of
memory space.

Example

A microprocessor with a 16-bit address bus uses memory in the top 8K of
memory space. What is the lowest address in this portion of memory
space?

Answer E000

Example

A microprocessor program that is 2K bytes long begins at address 1400H
in memory space. What is the ending address of the program?

Answer 1BFF

THE CONTROL BUS

In addition to the data bus and the address bus, microprocessors must also
have a set of control lines—both input control lines and output control

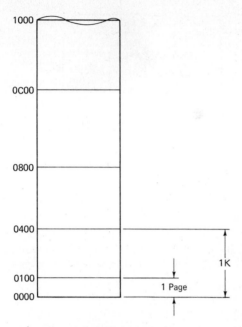

FIGURE 1–11
The 1K boundaries of memory are
shown here for the first 4K of memory
space. There are four pages of memory
in every 1K of memory space.

lines—that can be used to synchronize the operation of the microprocessor
to the operation of external circuitry. Collectively, these control lines are the
control bus of the microprocessor. You have already seen one example of a
control output line, namely the DBIN signal of Fig. 1-5. This signal is used
to indicate to external circuitry the status of the microprocessor bidirectional data bus.

    As another example of where control lines are required, suppose that
some external device needs to directly access the memory of a microprocessor system. In order to accomplish this *direct memory access* or
·DMA, there must exist some mechanism for effectively disconnecting the
microprocessor from its memory so that the external device can gain
control of the address bus and the data bus.

    A special control input is provided on many microprocessors to permit
DMA operation. This input is labeled HOLD in Fig. 1-12. A logic 1 signal on
the HOLD line indicates to the microprocessor that some external device is
requesting control of the address and data buses. In order to accommodate
this request, the microprocessor places its address and data bus outputs in
what is called a *tristate* condition, shown diagrammatically in Fig. 1-13.

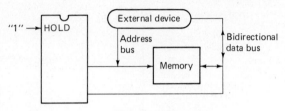

FIGURE 1–12
Direct memory access by an external device.

This effectively disconnects the microprocessor from the address and data buses.

Once the address and data bus outputs enter this tristate condition, the microprocessor in this example responds to the external device's HOLD request by issuing a hold acknowledge signal on the HLDA line shown in Fig. 1-13. HLDA is another example of a typical control output line of a microprocessor control bus. The external device is designed to wait for a logic 1 signal on the HLDA line before actually taking over the address and data bus. This communications protocol of making a request and then waiting for a response before proceeding is called *handshaking*. Handshaking protocols like this are very common in microprocessor systems.

Any given control signal of a control bus can be either *active high* or *active low*. In the case of the examples discussed above (DBIN, HOLD, and

FIGURE 1–13
An address line and bidirectional data bus line shown in the tristate condition when a logic 1 signal is applied to the HOLD input of the microprocessor.

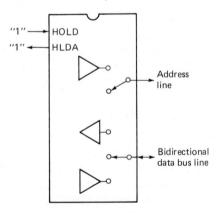

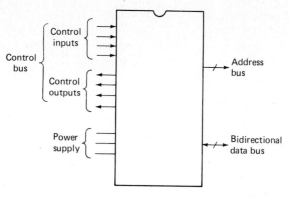

FIGURE 1-14
The generalized microprocessor.

HLDA), the signals are said to be active high because a logic 1 is used to indicate the active signal condition. If, for example, a logic 0 indicated that the data bus was in the input mode, then a bar would be placed over the signal name to indicate that it was in fact an active low signal. If this were the case, the control output would be labelled $\overline{\text{DBIN}}$ which is pronounced "dee bee in bar". The bar notation is very convenient for showing at a glance which control signals are active high and which are active low.

THE GENERAL MICROPROCESSOR

You are now prepared to formulate a generalized model of a microprocessor. As shown in Fig. 1-14 the microprocessor is a digital device with (1) a data bus, (2) an address bus, and (3) a control bus. The microprocessor is able to input information in the form of digital signals, process information according to a stored program, and output information in the form of digital signals. The stored program may in some cases reside in memory internal to the microprocessor itself. In other cases the program may be stored in external memory. In addition to the three major buses, the microprocessor requires one or more power-supply voltages to power its internal circuitry and provide a voltage reference for the microprocessor signal lines.

SUMMARY

Several new terms and conventions are used in microprocessor engineering. You should understand the meaning of data path width, bidirectional data bus, memory space, direct memory access, and handshaking protocol. You should know the definition of terms such as byte, nybble, and tristate. You should also be familiar with hexadecimal notation.

A generalized model for a microprocessor is a device with a data bus, address bus, and control bus. The size of the data and address bus, the nature of the control signals making up the control bus, and the power-supply requirements are all factors that differentiate the various microprocessors that are available today.

The next chapter will cover the details of microprocessor fabrication—the physical realization of the microprocessor itself. Then, in Chap. 3, you will be prepared to deal with several specific microprocessors in the context of the general microprocessor model developed in this chapter.

EXERCISES

(Answers to odd-numbered problems are given at the end of the book.)

1-1   Convert the following five binary numbers to hexadecimal numbers:

10111011,   11001011,   11000011,   10101010,
11110000.

1-2   Convert the following five binary numbers to octal numbers:

11111111,   01010101,   11000111,   00111110,
11000011.

1-3   Convert the following five octal numbers to binary numbers:

303,   77,   351,   62,   333.

1-4   Convert the following five octal numbers to hexadecimal numbers:

076,   377,   323,   111,   333.

1-5   Convert the following five hexadecimal numbers to octal numbers:

FF,   C3,   5A,   EE,   07.

1-6   Convert the following five hexadecimal numbers to binary numbers:

FF,   ABCD,   11,   C3,   06.

1-7   What is the size of the memory space for an 8-bit microprocessor with a 12-bit address word? (Answer in kilobytes.)

1-8   What is the size of the memory space for a 16-bit microprocessor with a 20-bit address word? (Answer in kilowords.)

1-9 For a microprocessor with 32K of contiguous memory beginning at location 0000H in memory space, what is the highest usable memory address? (Answer in hex notation.)

1-10 For a microprocessor with 48K of contiguous memory beginning at location 0000H in memory space, what is the highest usable memory address? (Answer in hex notation.)

1-11 For a microprocessor with 3K of contiguous memory beginning at address E400 in memory space, what is the highest usable memory address? (Answer in hex notation.)

1-12 For a microprocessor with 1K of contiguous memory beginning at location A000 in memory space, what is the highest usable memory address? (Answer in hex notation.)

1-13 How many kilowords of memory space are there between location B000 and BFFF inclusive?

1-14 How many kilowords of memory space are there between location E000 and E3FF inclusive?

1-15 A particular microprocessor system uses a hexadecimal number to indicate system status to an operator. Following an attempted disk write operation, for example, a two-digit hexadecimal number can indicate any combination of eight error conditions, as summarized in the table below:

Bit	Indication
7	Not ready
6	Write protect
5	Write fault
4	Record not found
3	CRC error
2	Lost data
1	Data request
0	Busy

If a disk write operation could not proceed because the disk was write-protected, what would the hexadecimal status word be to indicate this condition?

1-16   Referring again to the table of Exercise 1-15, what hexadecimal word would indicate a CRC (cyclic redundancy check) error?

1-17   What is the minimum number of lines required for a microprocessor control bus to specify eight distinct states?

1-18   What is the minimum number of lines required for a microprocessor control bus to specify 15 distinct states?

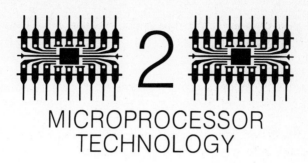

2

MICROPROCESSOR
TECHNOLOGY

Powerful, low-cost microprocessors are available today only because of the tremendous advances made in integrated-circuit technology in the past decade. The integrating process allows the economical fabrication of complex circuits, consisting of thousands of transistors, on tiny chips of silicon. An entire microprocessor circuit can be fabricated on a silicon chip that is only a few millimeters on a side. A photomicrograph of a silicone chip containing a microprocessor circuit is shown in Fig. 2-1. Before this chip can be used, however, it must be mounted in an IC package. The pins of the IC package must be electrically connected to the IC chip itself by means of small bonding wires, and the entire package must then be sealed. A picture showing a completely packaged microprocessor is given in Fig. 2-2.

The idea of using integrated-circuit technology to build microprocessors was first conceived by Dr. Ted Hoff at the Intel Corporation in 1969. Dr. Federico Faggin then led the design team at Intel to develop the world's first microprocessors. Since the introduction of the first microprocessor in 1971, advances in integrated-circuit technology have spelled further advances in microprocessors. Today, over one hundred different microprocessors are available, and six different IC technologies are used in the manufacturing of these microprocessors. An understanding of these technologies is important in both the selection and application of microprocessors.

A summary of the six major technologies used in the fabrication of microprocessors is given in Fig. 2-3 along with representative examples of each. As can be seen from this figure, microprocessor ICs may be built with either bipolar or MOS (metal-oxide-silicon) transistors. Bipolar microprocessors may use ECL, Schottky, or I²L circuitry. MOS microprocessors may use P-channel, N-channel, or CMOS circuitry. Each of these technolo-

19

FIGURE 2–1
8748 microprocessor chip photomicrograph. (*Intel Corporation.*)

gies offers a unique trade-off between the price and the performance of the microprocessor.

BIPOLAR TECHNOLOGY

The fastest microprocessors available today are built using bipolar integrated-circuit technology. In order to understand the differences among the various bipolar technologies, it is necessary first to review the operation of the basic bipolar transistor amplifier, shown in Fig. 2-4a. Since this is an inverting amplifier, the output is high when the input signal is low, and low when the input signal is high. If the input signal to this amplifier were a rectangular pulse, you would, ideally, expect the output signal to be an inverted rectangular pulse as shown in Fig. 2-4b. In reality, however, the output waveform may not be this ideal, as seen in an actual oscilloscope photograph in Fig. 2-5. This oscilloscope photograph illustrates two

FIGURE 2–2
A packaged 8748 microprocessor.
(*Intel Corporation.*)

FIGURE 2–3
Summary of microprocessor technologies with representative examples.

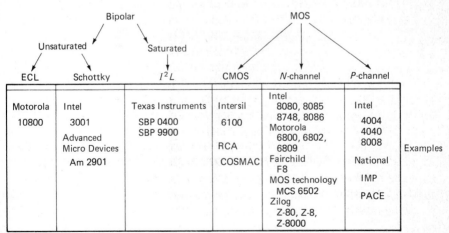

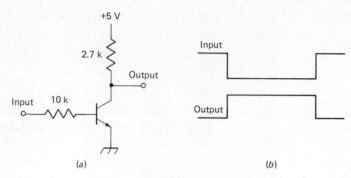

FIGURE 2-4
The basic *NPN* transistor amplifier.

nonideal effects in this simple bipolar transistor circuit that limit its speed of operation.

The first nonideal effect is the *saturation delay time*. This is the delay time from the falling edge of the input pulse to the beginning of the response in the output waveform. This saturation delay is caused by excess charge accumulating in the base region of the transistor when the input signal is high and the transistor is on and in saturation. This excess charge continues to supply collector current for a short period of time even after the input signal goes low.

The second nonideal effect is the *passive risetime* resulting in the

FIGURE 2-5
Oscilloscope photograph of input waveform and resultant output waveform for basic *NPN* transistor amplifier.

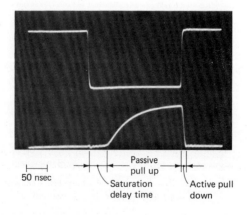

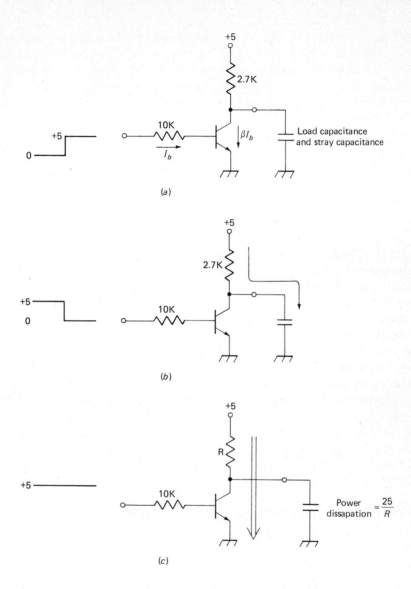

FIGURE 2–6

(*a*) The output waveform of this basic amplifier has a short falltime due to active pull-down. (*b*) The risetime of the output waveform is considerably longer due to passive pull-up. (*c*) The rise time of the output waveform can be appreciably shortened by decreasing the resistance of *R*, but at the expense of increased power dissipation when the transistor is on.

relatively slow risetime of the output waveform following the saturation delay. The falltime of the output, on the other hand, is relatively short. This occurs because the transistor is able to actively pull down the output with a collector current that is beta times the base current (where beta is the current gain of the transistor). As a result, any stray capacitance or load capacitance at the output is rapidly discharged (see Fig. 2-6a). When the transistor turns off, however, this capacitance must passively charge up through the collector resistor resulting in a slow waveform risetime (Fig. 2-6b). Quantitatively, this risetime is given by the formula

$$Risetime = 2.2RC$$

where the risetime is in nanoseconds, R is the collector resistance in kilohms, and C is the total load capacitance in picofarads.

The effects of saturation delay and passive risetime act to slow down the operation of the most simple bipolar transistor circuit. Since speed of operation is important in microprocessors, circuit designs had to be developed to ameliorate these effects. The most obvious way to eliminate the problem of saturation delay time is simply not to allow the transistors to go into saturation. One way this can be achieved is by connecting a Schottky diode from the base to the collector of the transistor (Fig. 2-7a). With this diode in place, the collector-base junction of the transistor is clamped so that it cannot be forward-biased, which is a necessary condition for saturation. A transistor with this special diode in place is called a *Schottky transistor* and has the special symbol shown in Fig. 2-7b.

The effectiveness of a Schottky-clamped transistor in reducing saturation delay time is clearly evident in the oscilloscope photograph of Fig. 2-8. Here, the input and output waveforms are shown for a circuit that is identical to the circuit of Fig. 2-4a except for the Schottky transistor used in place of the regular transistor. In this case, the saturation delay time is virtually eliminated. Schottky-clamped circuitry is now commonly used in bipolar integrated circuits designed for digital applications. Microproces-

FIGURE 2–7
The Schottky transistor. (a) A Schottky diode is connected from base to collector. (b) Equivalent schematic symbol.

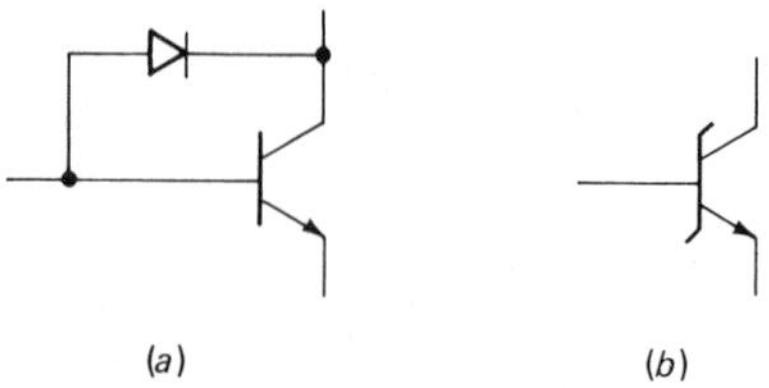

(a)   (b)

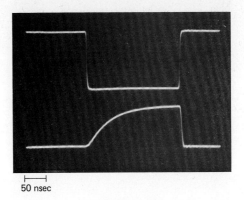

50 nsec

FIGURE 2-8
Input and output waveforms for a circuit
identical to that of Fig. 2-2 except that a
Schottky transistor is used. Note that
saturation delay time is greatly reduced.

sors such as the popular 2901 made by Advanced Micro Devices use
Schottky bipolar circuitry.

While Schottky-clamped circuitry provides one method for avoiding the
problems of saturation delay, another approach is to use circuitry in which

FIGURE 2-9
Basic pulse amplifier used in ECL microprocessors. (*a*) Basic ECL circuit.
(*b*) Basic circuit with output level-shifter.

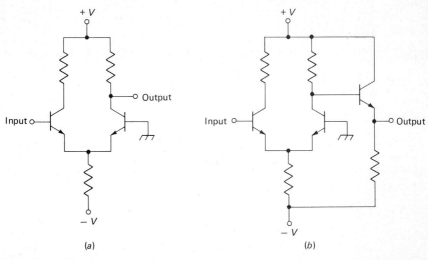

(*a*)   (*b*)

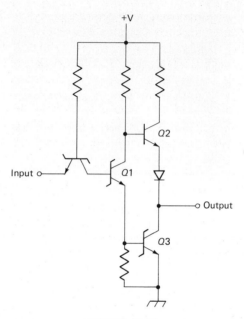

FIGURE 2–10
The basic pulse amplifier circuit used in
Schottky microprocessors. It provides
both active pull-up and active pull-down.
Transistors are Schottky-clamped to
avoid saturation delays.

the transistors are biased to operate only in their linear region. This is the
approach used in *emitter-coupled logic* (ECL). The basic ECL circuit is
shown in Fig. 2-9*a*. This same circuit is shown with a level-shifter at the
output in Fig. 2-9*b*. The fastest digital circuits in production today use ECL
designs, and this is the technology of choice in the largest computers
manufactured. ECL circuitry has also found limited application in microprocessor designs, most notably in the Motorola 10800 microprocessor.

The problem of a slow, passive risetime in the circuit of Fig. 2-4*a* can be
solved in a number of ways. One approach is simply to reduce the size of
the collector resistor. While this will, in fact, quicken the risetime of the
circuit, it has the undesirable effect of increasing the total power consumption of the circuit when the transistor is on (Fig. 2-6*c*). Quantitatively
this power dissipation is given by the formula

$$\text{Power dissipation} = \frac{V^2}{R}$$

where the power dissipation is in milliwatts, V is the supply voltage in volts, and R is the collector resistance in kilohms.

The technique most commonly used to avoid the problem of slow circuit risetime uses two transistors in a "totem pole" configuration. One transistor provides active pull-up; the other transistor provides active pull-down. In the circuit of Fig. 2-10, transistors Q2 and Q3 serve as the totem pole pair. Q1 is used as a phase inverter to assure that Q2 is off when Q3 is on and vice versa. Q1 and Q3 are Schottky-clamped transistors in this circuit. Transistor Q2 always operates in its linear region, and so it need not be a Schottky transistor.

An important capability in microprocessor circuitry is the ability to tristate an output. As described in Chap. 1, tristate outputs are effectively disconnected from the signal buses, allowing other devices to take control of these lines. To see how tristate capability can be added to the circuit of Fig. 2-10, refer to the circuit diagram shown in Fig. 2-11. Here, a signal to the tristate control input is used to turn off both Q2 and Q3 which serves to tristate the output.

FIGURE 2–11
The circuit of Fig. 2–10 can be modified for tristate output capability as shown. A logic 0 signal to the output enable control input will disable, or tristate, the output.

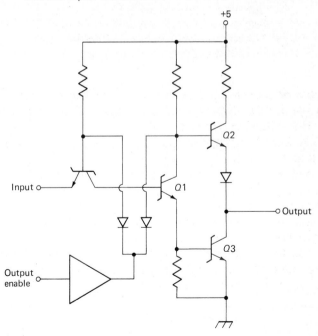

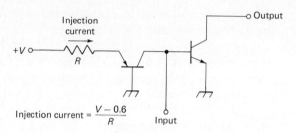

Injection current $= \dfrac{V - 0.6}{R}$

FIGURE 2–12
Basic I²L circuit is economical to manufacture.
Speed and power consumption of the circuit are
set by the magnitude of the injection current,
which is just equal to $(V - 0.6)/R$.

The newest bipolar technology to be applied to microprocessors is that
of *integrated injection logic* (I²L). I²L uses saturated transistors, and so the
speeds attainable are slower than those of Schottky or ECL circuitry. But I²L
does have other unique advantages.

The basic I²L circuit is shown in Fig. 2-12. When the input signal is high
(or open), the *injection current* flows through Q1 and turns on Q2. When the
input signal is low (at ground potential), the injection current is shorted to
ground, and Q2 turns off for lack of base current. An important feature of
this circuit is that the injection current is *programmable*: that is, the
magnitude of the injection current is set by the supply voltage V and the
series resistance R. The injection current is given by the formula

$$\text{Injection current} = \frac{V - 0.6}{R}$$

where the injection current is in milliamperes, V is in volts, and R is in
kilohms.

Since the user of an I²L microprocessor is able to set the injection
current, a design trade-off between speed of operation and power consumption can be made. When the injection current is small, the power
consumption is low, but the maximum speed of operation is reduced.
Higher injection currents permit higher-speed operation, but at the expense of power consumption. A chart showing the typical clock periods
attainable as a function of injection current for the SBP 9900 16-bit I²L
microprocessor is given in Fig. 2-13.

An unusual feature of I²L circuitry is its ability to be powered from a
supply voltage as low as 0.8 V. Since the performance characteristics are
set by the injection *current*, the actual voltage/resistance combination used
to attain that injection current can vary greatly. The relative voltage

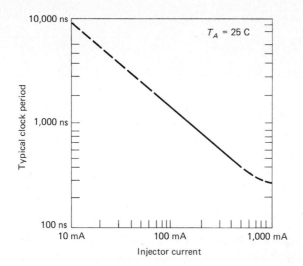

FIGURE 2–13
Clock period as a function of injection current for
the SBP 9900 microprocessor.

insensitivity of I²L circuitry and its programmable power consumption make this technology a particularly attractive choice in battery-powered applications.

MOS TECHNOLOGY

Most microprocessors being manufactured today use MOS transistors rather than bipolar transistors in their integrated circuitry. The main advantage of MOS technology over bipolar technology is its higher density. The higher density of MOS circuitry allows many more functions to be placed on a silicon chip of a given size than could be attained using bipolar circuitry.

There are two types of MOS transistors that can be used in MOS microprocessor circuitry. These are the *P-channel* transistors and the *N-channel* transistors. For the *P*-channel devices, the electrical carriers are "holes" in the semiconductor while for the *N*-channel devices, the carriers are electrons. The basic *P*-channel and *N*-channel amplifiers are shown in Fig. 2-14.

The earliest microprocessors used *P*-channel MOS technology. *P*-channel technology, however, has two major disadvantages. First, holes have a lower mobility in silicon than do electrons. As a result, *P*-channel transistors are inherently slower than *N*-channel devices. Second, referring

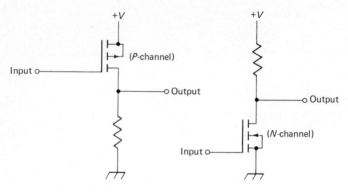

FIGURE 2-14
Basic *P*-channel and *N*-channel MOS amplifiers.

to Fig. 2-14, *P*-channel circuits provide active pull-up but *passive* pull-down of external loads. *N*-channel amplifiers, on the other hand, provide *active* pull-down, which is more effective in driving the TTL (transistor-transistor logic) interface circuits commonly used with microprocessors. While *P*-channel MOS technology provided the lowest-cost approach in early microprocessor designs, it is not used in new designs today.

N-channel technology is the most widely used technology in microprocessor fabrication today. The first *N*-channel microprocessor was the 8080 introduced in 1973. The original 8080 was designed for a maximum clock frequency of 2 MHz. Advances in *N*-channel technology now permit *N*-channel microprocessors to use clock rates as high as 10 MHz.

An important point to note in MOS microprocessor design is that the load "resistors" shown in Fig. 2-14 are actually MOS transistors used as resistors. *P*-channel and *N*-channel MOS transistors can be further categorized as either *depletion mode* or *enhancement mode* devices. Depletion-mode transistors are normally on and require a gate voltage to be turned off. Enhancement-mode devices are normally off and require a gate voltage in order to be turned on. Early *N*-channel microprocessors, such as the 8080, used enhancement-mode transistors as the load resistors. This has the disadvantage of requiring a separate power supply to provide gate voltage for the load devices. Newer MOS microprocessor designs use depletion-mode loads which have eliminated the need for an extra power-supply voltage. These processors can operate from a single 5-volt power supply (Fig. 2-15).

The third type of MOS transistor circuit used in microprocessors is the CMOS (complementary MOS) circuit of Fig. 2-16. The key advantage of this circuit is its use of complementary transistors (i.e., one *P*-channel and one *N*-channel device) for both active pull-up and active pull-down of the load.

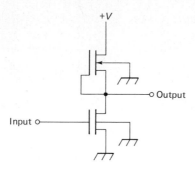

FIGURE 2–15
N-channel MOS amplifier stage
with a depletion-mode load is
the most common circuit configuration used in microprocessors
today. A depletion-mode MOS
transistor serves as the load "resistor." This permits microprocessor operation from a single supply voltage.

The power consumption of CMOS circuitry is very low. There is no path from
the power supply to ground since one of the two transistors is always off.
This is shown diagrammatically in Fig. 2-17. The major application of
CMOS microprocessors occurs when low power consumption is the
dominating design constraint.

FIGURE 2–16
Basic CMOS amplifier uses
both a *P*-channel and an *N*-
channel MOS transistor.

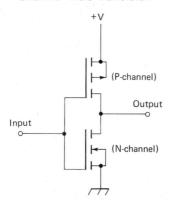

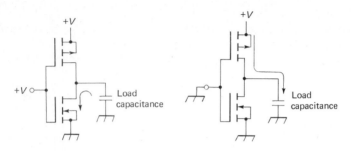

FIGURE 2–17
The CMOS amplifier provides both active pull-up and active
pull-down.

FIGURE 2–18
This CMOS SOS microprocessor from Hewlett-Packard uses CMOS technology on an insulating sapphire substrate.

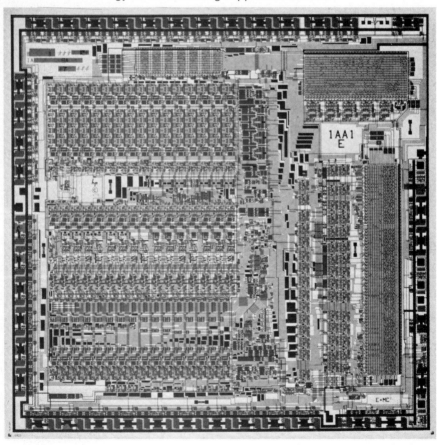

The speed of conventional CMOS circuitry is limited by substrate capacitances. To reduce the effect of these substrate capacitances, the newest MOS technology used in microprocessor fabrication employs an insulating substrate, usually sapphire, for the CMOS circuitry. This technology is called *silicon on sapphire* (SOS). The first CMOS SOS microprocessor was developed by the Hewlett-Packard company, and is shown in Fig. 2-18.

SUMMARY

The six integrated circuit technologies used in microprocessor fabrication are (1) ECL bipolar, (2) Schottky bipolar, (3) I²L bipolar, (4) complementary MOS, (5) *N*-channel MOS, and (6) *P*-channel MOS. The *N*-channel MOS process is the most widely used in the manufacture of microprocessors today. If either speed of operation, power consumption, or cost is a strongly dominant factor in a microprocessor application, however, other technologies should be considered. The fastest microprocessors available use either ECL or Schottky bipolar technology. The lowest power consumption is found in CMOS microprocessors. I²L microprocessors can operate with the lowest power-supply voltages and offer low-power operation if high speed is not required. CMOS microprocessors built on an insulating substrate provide both high-speed and low-power operation, but the cost of these microprocessors is high. The lowest-cost microprocessors available today use the *P*-channel process, although these are rapidly being replaced by *N*-channel microprocessors in most applications.

EXERCISES

2-1   What is the injection current for an I²L microprocessor with a 10-V power supply and a 100-Ω current limiting resistor?

2-2   What is the injection current for an I²L microprocessor with a 5-V power supply and a 33-Ω current limiting resistor?

2-3   What clock frequency can be used with the SBP 9900 microprocessor for an injection current of 500 mA? (Refer to Fig. 2-13.)

2-4   What clock frequency can be used with the SBP 9900 microprocessor when the power-supply voltage is 30 V and the current limiting resistor is 270 Ω?

2-5   What types of applications would require an ECL microprocessor?

2-6   What types of applications would require a Schottky bipolar micro-processor?

2-7   What types of applications would require a I²L microprocessor?

2-8   What types of applications would require a CMOS microprocessor?

2-9   What types of applications would require an NMOS (N-channel MOS) microprocessor?

2-10 What types of applications would require a PMOS (P-channel MOS) microprocessor?

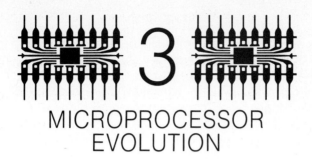

MICROPROCESSOR EVOLUTION

Since the introduction of the first microprocessor in 1971, microprocessor performance has increased impressively. Improved performance has been achieved in three ways. First, more advanced technologies (as described in Chap. 2) have been employed in microprocessor fabrication. Second, the detailed logic design or *architecture* of the microprocessor has improved. And third, more memory and I/O interfaces have been included on the microprocessor chip itself, thus reducing the required number of external components. In brief, microprocessors are evolving toward the ideal microprocessor described in Chap. 1: a device with only inputs, outputs, and a resident program.

Of course, the ideal microprocessor will only be approached asymptotically. As an engineer, you must learn to design with *real* devices. For microprocessors, this means you must learn *hardware design*—the physical implementation of external circuitry required to take full advantage of the microprocessor—as well as *software design*—the formulation of the detailed steps of the microprocessor program. As microprocessors have evolved, both hardware and software design have actually become *easier* to implement for systems with comparable capabilities.

To see how microprocessors have evolved, six specific examples of microprocessors will be discussed in this chapter: the 8008, 8080, Z80, 8748, Z8000, and 8086. The 8008 and 8080 are 8-bit microprocessors discussed primarily for historical perspective. The Z80 and 8748 are current 8-bit microprocessors. The Z8000 and the 8086 herald the beginning of high-performance 16-bit microprocessors. Detailed information on each of these microprocessors can be found in the manufacturers' literature cited at the end of this chapter.

THE 8008

The 8008 is an 8-bit, first-generation microprocessor that was introduced in January 1972. It is actually the second of the first-generation processors, following the 4004, a 4-bit processor introduced in November 1971. The 8008 is fabricated using the *P*-channel MOS process, and is compact as microprocessors go, being packaged in an 18-pin *dual in-line package* (DIP). The pinout is shown in Fig. 3-1.

Referring to Fig. 3-1, we see that eight pins of the microprocessor are used as an 8-bit bidirectional data bus. Two power-supply voltages are

FIGURE 3–1
(*a*) Pin configuration. (*b*) Block diagram.

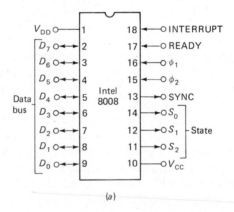

(*a*)

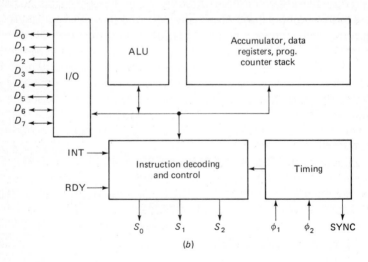

(*b*)

required: V_{DD} is −9 V and V_{CC} is +5 V. Two clock signals, ϕ1 and ϕ2, are also required. Three lines of the microprocessor (S0, S1, and S2) are used to indicate the state of the microprocessor to external circuitry. The SYNC output is used to indicate the beginning of each machine cycle when new information is put out on the state lines. An important feature of the 8008 is the READY line which can be used to temporarily stop the operation of the microprocessor by applying a logic 0 signal to this input. Finally, the 8008 has an interrupt input that can be used to change the course of execution of the microprocessor program. External hardware can be used to put a logic 1 signal on this input to effect an interrupt. A summary of the 8008 pinout is shown in Fig. 3-2.

The 8008 has no provision for program storage on the microprocessor chip itself. The microprocessor program must be stored in memory external to the microprocessor, which can be addressed and read by the microprocessor. But the 8008 has no address lines. How can this be?

Quite simply, address information (the coded sequence of bits used to select an external memory location) is *multiplexed* on the 8-bit bidirectional data bus. At the beginning of each machine cycle requiring a memory reference (either to read from or write to memory), address information is put on the "data" bus at the beginning of the machine cycle. This address information must be saved or *latched* by external circuitry. Only then does the actual data transfer occur on the data bus. The address put out by the 8008 is 14 bits long. First, the eight low-order bits are put out and externally latched. Then, the six high-order bits are put out and externally latched. The 8008 is thus able to address 2^{14} or 16,384 separate memory locations.

The architecture of the 8008 is shown in Fig. 3-3. Although it is not necessary to understand this diagram in complete detail at this time, several points should be mentioned. First, note that there is memory space on the chip that can be used for data storage (although not for program storage). This memory space is organized as seven 8-bit registers (registers A, B, C, D, E, H, and L). The contents of these registers may be

FIGURE 3–2
Summary of 8008 pinout.

Address	Data	Control Bus		Power supply, V
		Inputs	Outputs	
14 bits multiplexed	8-bit bidirectional	Interrupt	Sync	+5
on data bus		Ready	S0	−9
		ϕ1	S1	
		ϕ2	S2	

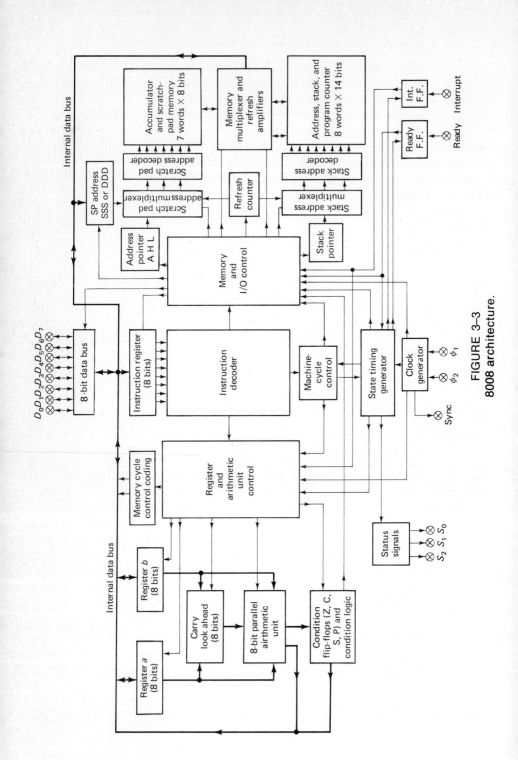

FIGURE 3-3
8008 architecture.

modified or interrogated by the microprocessor program. The A register is also called the *accumulator* since the result of arithmetic operations is normally stored here. Also note that the 8008 has eight internal 14-bit storage locations. One of these is called the *program counter* (PC) and is used to store the address of the instruction in external memory that is currently being executed by the microprocessor. The remaining seven 14-bit locations comprise what is called the *stack.* If, during the course of the microprocessor program, a subroutine call instruction is encountered, the current value of the program counter is stored in the stack to save the *return location* before the processor branches to the subroutine. Since there are seven stack locations, there can be a maximum of just seven nested subroutines in an 8008 program.

One measure of performance of a microprocessor is the number of different program instructions in its repertoire. The number of instructions in its instruction set is one measure of the power of the instruction set. For the case of the 8008 there are a total of 48 distinct instructions that comprise the instruction set.

The 8008 is a very low-cost microprocessor, but the low cost is achieved at the expense of performance. As discussed in Chap. 2, *P*-channel technology is inherently slower than other technologies. And multiplexing address information on the data bus, rather than having separate address lines, slows performance even further. The minimum time required to execute a single program instruction with the standard 8008 is 20 µs.

THE 8080

The 8080 was the first of the second-generation microprocessors, and was introduced in November 1973. Today, it is one of the most widely used microprocessors in the world. The 8080 is fabricated using the *N*-channel MOS process. It is packaged in a 40-pin DIP as shown in Fig. 3-4. The functions of these pins can be divided into five categories:

1. address bus

2. bidirectional data bus

3. power supply

4. control bus inputs

5. control bus outputs

The 8080 has 16 address lines and is thus able to address up to 2^{16} or 65,536 bytes of memory. The 8080 also has an 8-bit bidirectional data bus.

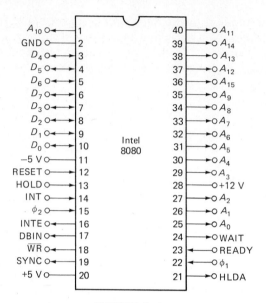

FIGURE 3–4
8080 pin configuration.

The DBIN output (pin 17) is used to signal whether the data bus is in the input mode (DBIN = 1) or the output mode (DBIN = 0). Three power-supply voltages are required: +12 V at 40 mA, +5 V at 60 mA, and −5 V at 10 mA. All power-supply voltages are with reference to ground (pin 2). Six pins of the 8080 are used as control inputs. There are two clock inputs, the HOLD input, the READY input, the interrupt request (INT) input, and the RESET input.

Two clock signals, ϕ1 (pin 22) and ϕ2 (pin 15), are required by the 8080 for internal sequencing and timing. These two clock signals are nonoverlapping, 12-V pulse trains that must meet specific timing requirements. Circuitry to generate these clock waveforms is described in Chap. 4.

The HOLD input (pin 13) is held at logic 0 during normal operation of the 8080 microprocessor. To perform direct memory access (DMA), the HOLD input is raised to a logic 1 level to request that the processor enter a hold state. In the hold state, the processor ceases activity, and the data and address lines are in their high-impedance (tristate) mode.

The READY input (pin 23) is held at logic 1 during normal operation of the 8080. A logic 0 signal is applied to this input to request that the processor enter a wait state. Once in the wait state, the processor ceases activity until the READY input returns to logic 1.

One use of the READY input is in synchronizing the 8080 with slow memory or peripheral devices. After an address is put out on the address bus prior to a memory read, for example, the 8080 interrogates the READY line to see if the memory is prepared to respond with the desired byte of data. For the case of memories with slow access times, READY will be held low at this point, and continue to be held low, until valid data are on the data bus.

One difference between the hold state and the wait state is that the hold state can only be entered following the completion of an instruction of the microprocessor program. The wait state, on the other hand, is entered during the middle of an instruction execution, just after new address information is put on the address bus. A second difference is that in the hold state, the data bus and address bus are in their tristate mode while in the wait state they are not.

The interrupt request input is pin 14. While the 8080 is executing a program, it is possible to interrupt the program execution and branch to a new program. This interruption of program execution is initiated by a logic 1 signal on the interrupt request (INT) input. The 8080 will not acknowledge an interrupt request while in the hold state. It will also not acknowledge an interrupt unless its internal *interrupt enable (INTE) flip-flop* is set. This flip-flop can be set and reset by the program that the 8080 executes.

The RESET input is pin 12. During program execution, the RESET input to the 8080 is held at logic 0. To reset the 8080, and to begin program execution at location 0000H in memory, the RESET input must be held at logic 1 for at least three clock cycles. Program execution begins at location 0000H when the signal to the RESET input returns to logic 0. The interrupt enable and hold acknowledge (HLDA) flip-flops (described below) are also reset.

The 8080 control bus has six outputs: DBIN, INTE, SYNC, $\overline{WR}$, WAIT, and HLDA. The DBIN output is pin 17 and is used to signal to external circuitry that the 8-bit bidirectional data bus is either in the input mode (DBIN = 1) or in the output mode (DBIN = 0).

The interrupt enable (INTE) output, pin 16, indicates the state of the internal interrupt enable flip-flop. This flip-flop may be set or reset by the enable interrupt or disable interrupt instructions of the microprocessor program. When INTE = 0, the microprocessor will not acknowledge an interrupt request input.

The SYNC output is pin 19. One use of the bidirectional data bus of the 8080 is to output status information at the beginning of each machine cycle. The SYNC pulse appears at the beginning of each machine cycle and is used to indicate the presence of status information on the data bus.

The write ($\overline{WR}$) output is pin 18. The signal is used to indicate when valid output data is available on the data bus. When data is output to external

| Address | Data | Control Bus | | Power supply, V |
		Inputs	Outputs	
16 lines	8 bidirectional	Ø1	DBIN	+5
		Ø2	INTE	+12
		HOLD	SYNC	−5
		READY	$\overline{WR}$	
		INT	WAIT	
		RESET	HLDA	

FIGURE 3–5
Summary of 8080 pinout.

memory or to an output device, the $\overline{WR}$ line goes from $\overline{WR} = 1$ to $\overline{WR} = 0$ when the output is valid.

The WAIT output is pin 24 and is used to indicate when the processor is in a wait state. WAIT = 1 when the processor is in a wait state; otherwise, WAIT = 0. There are two ways by which the wait state can be requested. One way is by applying a logic 0 signal to the READY input. The second way is by execution of the HALT instruction in the microprocessor program.

The hold acknowledge (HLDA) output is pin 21 and goes to logic 1 to indicate that the processor has acknowledged a HOLD request input. The data lines and address lines will subsequently go to their high-impedance state.

A summary of the 8080 pinout is shown in Fig. 3-5.

In addition to the six output control lines emanating from the 8080 microprocessor itself, eight additional bits of control information are output on the data bus at the beginning of each machine cycle. This is the *status* information that is used as follows:

D0: INTA, or interrupt acknowledge, indicates that the processor has responded to an interrupt on the INT control line.

D1: $\overline{WO}$ indicates by a logic 0 that the processor is in a memory write or an output cycle.

D2: STACK indicates that the processor is doing either a stack read or write operation.

D3: HLTA, or halt acknowledge, signifies that the processor has come to a stop as a result of executing a HALT instruction.

D4: OUT indicates that data is being output to an output port.

D5: M1 indicates that the processor is doing an op code (instruction) fetch from memory.

D6: INP indicates that data is being input from an input port.

D7: MEMR signifies a memory read operation.

Even a minimal 8080 microprocessor system requires an external *status latch* to store this status information at the beginning of each machine cycle.

The architecture of the 8080 is shown in Fig. 3-6. Like the 8008, there are seven 8-bit registers (including the accumulator). There is a 16-bit program counter (compared to a 14-bit PC in the 8008). But where is the stack? Unlike the 8008, the 8080 uses an *external* stack rather than an internal stack. A 16-bit register, called the *stack pointer* (SP), keeps track of the location of the stack in external memory. A key advantage of this technique is that the size of the stack is not limited by the number of stack locations on the microprocessor chip itself.

The 8080 also has a more powerful instruction set than the 8008 with a total of 78 instructions. These 78 instructions include the 46 used in the 8008. By using *N*-channel technology and separate address lines, the 8080 instruction time (for the standard 8080) is 2 μs: a factor of ten faster than the 8008.

THE Z80

The first of the third-generation microprocessors is the Z80, introduced in April 1976. By using depletion-mode load, *N*-channel MOS fabrication, only a single +5-V power supply is required for the microprocessor. Only a single +5-V external clock signal is required. Additional control output signals are generated by the Z80 which eliminate the need to multiplex status information on the data bus, as is done with the 8080. The Z80 is contained in the same style 40-pin DIP that is used for the 8080. The pinout is shown in Fig. 3-7. Again, each terminal of the microprocessor can be categorized into one of five categories.

The Z80 has 16 address lines, and, like the 8080, is able to address 64K of memory. The Z80 also has an 8-bit bidirectional data bus. But, unlike the standard 8080, the Z80 requires just a single +5-V supply (pin 11) with respect to ground (pin 29). The Z80 can use a single supply in this way because of the depletion-mode load technology used to fabricate the IC.

The Z80 has six control inputs. These are the clock input (pin 6), the

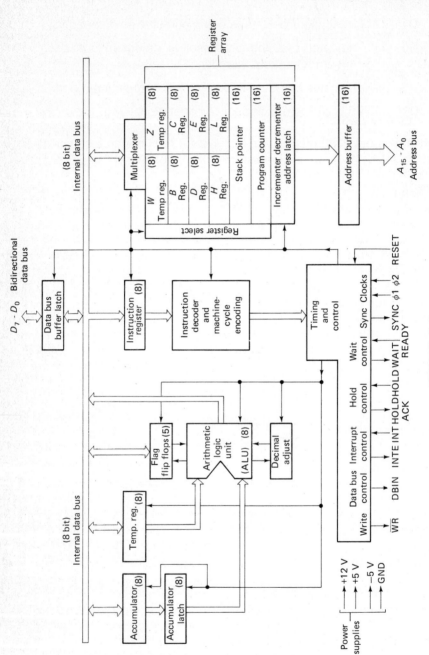

FIGURE 3–6
8080 architecture.

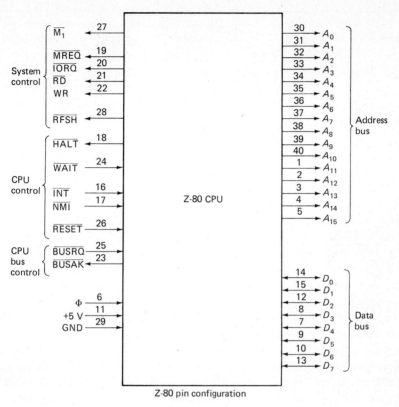

Z-80 pin configuration

FIGURE 3–7
Z80 pin configuration.

interrupt request input (pin 16), the nonmaskable interrupt request input (pin 17), the wait request input (pin 24), the bus request input (pin 25), and the reset input (pin 26).

The clock input requires a single 5-V pulse train. The detailed timing requirements are dependent upon the specific model of Z80 used (e.g., the high-speed or low-speed version) and can be found in the manufacturer's specification sheet. The interrupt request ($\overline{\text{INT}}$) is analogous to the INT line of the 8080 except that the request is initiated by an active low (logic 0) signal. This is indicated by the bar over the abbreviation for the input, that is, $\overline{\text{INT}}$ (pronounced interrupt bar). The nonmaskable interrupt input ($\overline{\text{NMI}}$) is similar to INT except that this input cannot be disabled by software instructions. The $\overline{\text{WAIT}}$ request is analogous to the READY line of the 8080. The bus request ($\overline{\text{BUSRQ}}$) is analogous to the HOLD line of the 8080. The $\overline{\text{RESET}}$ input is analogous to the RESET input of the 8080. Again this input is active low.

		Control Bus		
Address	Data	Inputs	Outputs	Power supply, V
16 lines	8-bit bidirectional	CLOCK	$\overline{\text{HALT}}$	
		$\overline{\text{INT}}$	$\overline{\text{MREQ}}$	
		$\overline{\text{NMI}}$	$\overline{\text{IORQ}}$	
		$\overline{\text{WAIT}}$	$\overline{\text{RD}}$	
		$\overline{\text{BUSRQ}}$	$\overline{\text{WR}}$	
		$\overline{\text{RESET}}$	$\overline{\text{BUSAK}}$	
			$\overline{\text{M1}}$	
			$\overline{\text{RFSH}}$	

FIGURE 3–8
Summary of Z80 pinout.

The Z80 has eight control output lines. The $\overline{\text{HALT}}$ output (pin 18) is analogous to the WAIT output of the 8080. The $\overline{\text{MREQ}}$ output (pin 19) goes low (as indicated by the bar) to signal that the address bus holds a valid address for a memory read or write operation. The $\overline{\text{IORQ}}$ output (pin 20) goes low to signal that the address bus holds a valid address for a I/O read or write operation. $\overline{\text{RD}}$ (pin 21) goes low to signal a memory or I/O read operation. $\overline{\text{WR}}$ (pin 22) goes low to signal a memory or I/O write operation. The $\overline{\text{BUSAK}}$ signal (pin 23) is analogous to the HLDA signal of the 8080. $\overline{\text{M1}}$ (pin 27) is used to indicate that the current machine cycle is the op code fetch cycle of an instruction execution. The $\overline{\text{RFSH}}$ (refresh bar) output (pin 28) has no counterpart in the 8080. This output is used as a control signal to simplify the refresh circuitry required with dynamic memory.

A summary of the Z80 pinout is shown in Fig. 3-8.

The internal architecture of the Z80 is very similar to that of the 8080 with the most striking difference being that there are over twice as many internal registers, as shown in Fig. 3-9. The instruction set of the Z80 consists of 158 instructions, including the 78 instructions of the 8080. Operating with a 4-MHz clock, the Z80 has a minimum instruction execution time of 1 μs.

THE 8748

A dramatic step in the evolution of microprocessors occurred with the introduction of the 8748 in February 1977. The remarkable feature of this microprocessor is that it contains 1024 bytes of programmable memory on

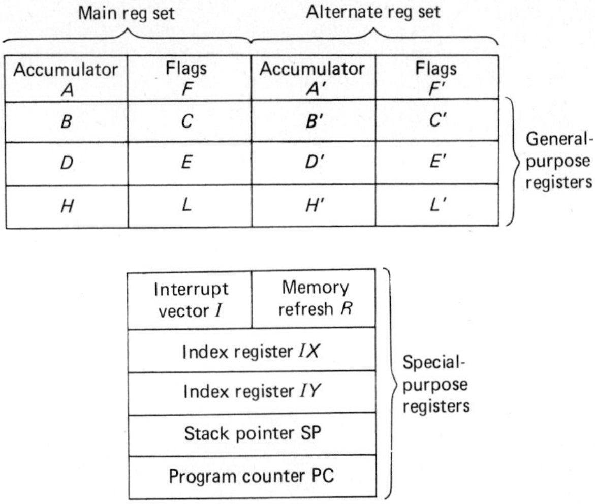

	Main reg set		Alternate reg set	
	Accumulator A	Flags F	Accumulator A'	Flags F'
	B	C	B'	C'
	D	E	D'	E'
	H	L	H'	L'

General-purpose registers

Interrupt vector I	Memory refresh R
Index register IX	
Index register IY	
Stack pointer SP	
Program counter PC	

Special-purpose registers

FIGURE 3–9
Z80 register configuration.

the same chip as the microprocessor itself. The 8748 is packaged in a conventional 40-pin DIP, but is covered with a transparent quartz lid. A user can shine intense ultraviolet (UV) light through this lid to erase the stored program, and subsequently reprogram the memory of the microprocessor.

Figure 3-10 shows the 8748 in its 40-pin package. Pins 12 to 19 form an 8-bit bidirectional data bus. There are two 8-bit bidirectional I/O ports (P10 through P17, and P20 through P27). Only a single 5-V supply is required for operation. The chip has its own internal clock circuit requiring just a crystal connected from pin 2 to pin 3.

There is no separate address bus for the 8748. Should you wish to expand the system beyond the memory internal to the 8748, however, address information is multiplexed over the data bus at the beginning of each machine cycle. An additional 4 bits of address information are available on the four low-order bits of port 2. Thus, there is a total of 12 bits of address information allowing the direct addressing of 4K of memory.

There are six control inputs to the 8748. T0 and T1 (pins 1 and 39) are software-testable, single-bit input ports. There is an interrupt line (pin 6), a reset line (pin 4), and a ready line (pin 5). The sixth control input, external access (EA), forces the 8748 to access external, rather than internal, program memory. This is useful primarily in system debugging.

There are four control outputs for the 8748. $\overline{RD}$ indicates a read from the data bus while $\overline{WR}$ indicates a write (or output) operation on the data bus. The ALE (address latch enable) signal is used to indicate that address

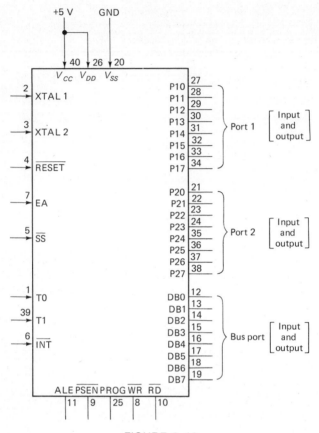

FIGURE 3–10
8748 pin configuration.

information is on the data bus so that it can be saved in an external latch. Finally the program store enable signal indicates that the current read operation (indicated by $\overline{RD}$ being logic 0) is fetching the next byte of the microprocessor program.

The 8748 microprocessor is built using N-channel MOS circuitry and is one of a family of processors having similar capability. A summary of the microprocessors in this family is given in Table 3-1. The 8048, for example, is a mask-programmed version of the 8748 that is programmed at the time of manufacturing and is not user programmable. A CMOS version of the 8048 is also available primarily for battery-powered applications. The 8748, with its on-chip memory and I/O capacity, begins to approach the ideal of a single-chip computer. A summary of the 8748 pinout is given in Fig. 3-11.

TABLE 3-1
Members of the 8748 Family of Microprocessors

	8021	8035	8039	8048	8049	8748
Resident program memory (bytes)	1K ROM	None	None	1K ROM	2K ROM	1K EPROM
Resident RAM memory (bytes)	64	64	128	64	128	64
Number of I/O lines	21	27	27	27	27	27
Number of IC pins	28	40	40	40	40	40
	Lowest cost					Highest cost

THE 8086

The 8086, introduced in June 1978, is the first of a high-performance generation of 16-bit microprocessors. The 8086 comes in a 40-pin dual in-line package and is manufactured using a high-speed N-channel MOS process (under the trade name of HMOS). The 8086 is able to directly address 1 megabyte (1024) kilobytes of external memory. Memory is organized as a low bank (data bits D0–D7) and a high bank (data bits D8 to D15). These banks each contain 512 bytes of memory and are addressed in parallel by the processor address lines A1 to A19. The 16-bit data path width of the 8086, its high-speed operation, and the large directly addressable memory space make this microprocessor ideal for applications requiring high system throughput. Throughput is further enhanced by a resident 6-byte look-ahead instruction queue.

The 6-byte lookahead instruction queue works in the following way (Fig.

FIGURE 3–11
Summary of 8748 pinout.

Address	Data	Control bus		Power supply, V
		Inputs	Outputs	
12 Bits, multi-	Three 8-bit	T0	$\overline{RD}$	
plexed on	bidirectional	T1	$\overline{WR}$	
data bus and	ports	$\overline{INTERRUPT}$	ALE	
output port			$\overline{PSEN}$	
		$\overline{RESET}$		
		$\overline{SS}$		
		EA		

3-12). While the 8086 is internally decoding the current instruction, the processor's bus interface unit (BIU) fetches the contents of the next sequential memory addresses (up to six, maximum) and loads them into the queue. Assuming that the current instruction is not a branch instruction, the next instruction is immediately available to the processor's execution

FIGURE 3–12
8086 architecture.

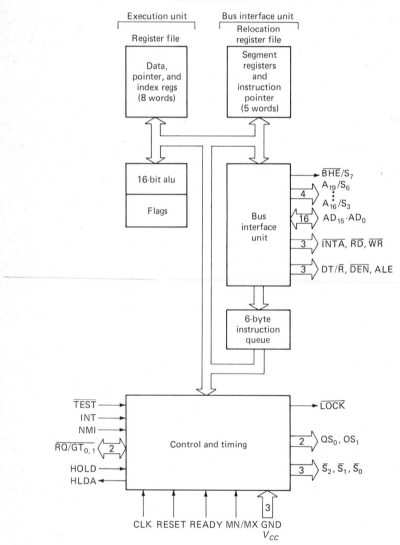

unit (EU) upon completion of the current instruction without the need for a delaying memory access. If the current instruction is a branch instruction, the next instruction is fetched from memory.

The detailed pinout of the 8086 is shown in Fig. 3-13. A single 5-V power supply is required to run the microprocessor. The bidirectional data bus is 16 bits wide (pins 2 to 16 and pin 39). The address bus is 20 bits wide with the low order 16 bits multiplexed on the data bus. The 20-bit wide address bus permits the direct access of 1 megabyte of memory from address 00000H to FFFFFH.

Many of the lines of the 8086 control bus are similar to those of microprocessors discussed above. The clock input (CLK) accepts a 5-V clock pulse train as high as 8 MHz in frequency. The 8086, like the Z-80 processor, has both a nonmaskable interrupt request input line (NMI) and a maskable interrupt request line (INTR). The READY line is similar to that of the 8080 in that it is used to stop the processor in the middle of a machine cycle. The RESET line is different, however, in that following a logic 1 reset signal, the 8086 processor begins program execution at location FFFF0H in memory space rather than at location 00000H. $\overline{\text{TEST}}$ is a control input the state of which can be tested in software by the *wait for test* instruction; if the $\overline{\text{TEST}}$ input is low, execution continues, otherwise the processor idles until the input does go low. The $\overline{\text{RD}}$ control output is analogous to the

FIGURE 3–13
8086 pin configuration.

	8086	
GND ⊏ 1		40 ⊐ V_{cc}
AD14 ⊏ 2		39 ⊐ AD15
AD13 ⊏ 3		38 ⊐ A16/S3
AD12 ⊏ 4		37 ⊐ A17/S4
AD11 ⊏ 5		36 ⊐ A18/S5
AD10 ⊏ 6		35 ⊐ A19/S6
AD9 ⊏ 7		34 ⊐ $\overline{\text{BHE}}$/S7
AD8 ⊏ 8		33 ⊐ MN/$\overline{\text{MX}}$
AD7 ⊏ 9		32 ⊐ $\overline{\text{RD}}$
AD6 ⊏ 10		31 ⊐ $\overline{\text{RQ}}$/$\overline{\text{GT0}}$ (HOLD)
AD5 ⊏ 11		30 ⊐ $\overline{\text{RQ}}$/$\overline{\text{GT1}}$ (HLDA)
AD4 ⊏ 12		29 ⊐ $\overline{\text{LOCK}}$ ($\overline{\text{WR}}$)
AD3 ⊏ 13		28 ⊐ $\overline{\text{S2}}$ (M/$\overline{\text{IO}}$)
AD2 ⊏ 14		27 ⊐ $\overline{\text{S1}}$ (DT/$\overline{\text{R}}$)
AD1 ⊏ 15		26 ⊐ $\overline{\text{S0}}$ ($\overline{\text{DEN}}$)
AD0 ⊏ 16		25 ⊐ QS0 (ALE)
NMI ⊏ 17		24 ⊐ QS1 ($\overline{\text{INTA}}$)
INTR ⊏ 18		23 ⊐ $\overline{\text{TEST}}$
CLK ⊏ 19		22 ⊐ READY
GND ⊏ 20		21 ⊐ RESET

corresponding signal of the Z80, indicating either a memory read or an input port operation.

Several output control lines of the 8086 are multiplexed on pins 34 to 38 of the processor. Since the 20 address lines of the 8086 are latched externally, address information need appear only at the beginning of a machine cycle (during what is known as the T1 state) when it is latched externally. One of the control output lines, $\overline{BHE}$, also appears only during T1. When $\overline{BHE}$ is low during T1 this signifies that the high byte of the data bus (D8 to D15) will be used for data transfer during the subsequent states of that machine cycle. Similarly address line A0 being low during T1 signifies that the low-order byte of the data bus (D0 to D7) will be used for data transfer during the subsequent states of that machine cycle. In other words, the entire 16-bit data bus is used for data transfer in a machine cycle only when both $\overline{BHE}$ and A0 are at logic 0 during T1 of that machine cycle. Since the address information and $\overline{BHE}$ information appears only during T1, the 21 lines of the processor bearing this information are all free for other purposes during the subsequent states of the machine cycle. As discussed above, 16 of the 21 lines are used for the bidirectional data bus. The remaining five lines are used for the five status lines S3 to S7.

To further add to the flexibility of configuring the 8086 processor, the remaining eight lines of the control bus (pins 24 to 31) can each serve one of two different functions depending on whether the processor is in minimum mode or maximum mode. The signal applied to the $MN/\overline{MX}$ control input line (pin 33) selects one of these two modes. When the $MN/\overline{MX}$ line is high the processor is in minimum mode and the eight control lines are used as follows. $\overline{INTA}$ goes low to acknowledge an interrupt, similar to the INTA status bit of the 8080. ALE is a control signal that appears during T1 and is used to strobe the address and $\overline{BHE}$ latches. If a bidirectional bus driver is used on the data bus (such as an 8286), $\overline{DEN}$ is used to enable the outputs of the drivers and DT/$\overline{R}$ is used to set the direction of the bus drivers. M/$\overline{IO}$ distinguishes a memory cycle from a I/O cycle, much like $\overline{IORQ}$ of the Z80. $\overline{WR}$ goes low to indicate a write operation either to memory or to an output port. Finally HOLD and HLDA are used just as on the 8080 to initiate and acknowledge a DMA operation.

When the $MN/\overline{MX}$ line is held low, the 8086 is in the maximum mode. In this mode QS0 and QS1 are two status bits used to provide information about the status of the internal instruction queue of the processor. Status bits $\overline{S0}$, $\overline{S1}$, and $\overline{S2}$ are used to encode information that, in minimum mode, appears on pins 24 to 29. These three status bits are normally decoded by an 8288 bus controller. The three remaining lines are used primarily in multiprocessor applications. $\overline{LOCK}$ is an output that is under control of the program that can be used to lock out other processors from gaining control

Address	Data	Control bus		Power supply
		Inputs	Outputs	
20 bits multiplexed	16 bits,	NMI	S0-S7	5 V
on data bus and	bidirectional	INTR	$\overline{BHE}$	
control bus		CLK	$\overline{RD}$	
		READY	QS0	
		RESET	QS1	
		$\overline{TEST}$	HLDA	
		MN/MX	$\overline{GT0}$	
		$\overline{RQ}$	$\overline{GT1}$	

FIGURE 3–14
Summary of 8086 pinout.

of the bus. The request/grant pins are used by other processors to force the active processor into a HOLD state in order to turn over control of the bus. $\overline{RQ}/\overline{GT0}$ has priority over $\overline{RQ}/\overline{GT1}$.

A summary of the 8086 pinout by function is given in Fig. 3-14. Although the 8086 evolved from the 8080 microprocessor, in many applications the 8086 will show an order of magnitude improvement in performance over that of its venerable ancestor.

THE Z8000

Like the 8068, the Z8000 is a 16-bit processor. The Z8000 is available either in a 40-pin package or a 48-pin package. The 40-pin Z8000 is able to address 64K of memory; the 48-pin model is able to address 8 megabytes of memory.

The detailed pinout of the Z8000 is shown in Fig. 3-15. Like the 8086, the 16 low-order address lines (A0 to A15) are multiplexed on the 16-bit bidirectional data bus. The address strobe signal $(\overline{AS})$ goes low at the beginning of a machine cycle to indicate that the address information is valid. Similarly $\overline{DS}$ serves as a data strobe and $\overline{MREQ}$ signifies a memory request. Seven lines of the output control bus are used to indicate processor status: ST0-ST3, WORD/$\overline{BYTE}$, NORMAL/$\overline{SYSTEM}$, and READ/$\overline{WRITE}$. The $\overline{WAIT}$ control input can be used to synchronize the processor to slow memory or I/O devices and the $\overline{STOP}$ line can be used to stop the processor when single-stepping through a program. The $\overline{BUSRQ}$ and $\overline{BUSAK}$ line serve the same function here as on the Z80 processor; a DMA request is made by a logic 0 signal on the $\overline{BUSRQ}$ input and the processor responds with a logic 0 signal on the control output line, $\overline{BUSAK}$.

There are three interrupt lines on the Z8000. $\overline{NMI}$ is a nonmaskable interrupt. $\overline{VI}$ is a maskable vectored interrupt. $\overline{NVI}$ is a maskable nonvec-

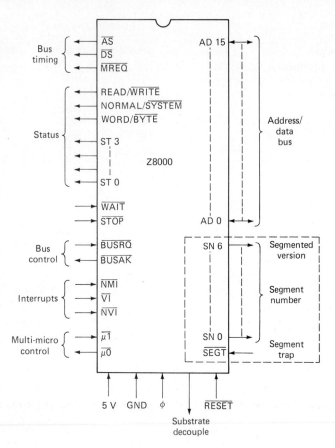

FIGURE 3–15
Z8000 pin configuration.

tored interrupt. A vectored interrupt can cause the processor to branch to any one of several memory locations to service the interrupt. A nonvectored interrupt causes a branch to a fixed location. The Z8000 also has two control lines named μI and $\overline{\mu O}$ (micro in and micro out) designed to synchronize multiple microprocessors in a multiprocessor system.

The 48-pin version of the Z8000 includes 7 additional address lines (SN0 to SN6). These 7 lines can specify one of 128 different memory segments. Since each segment can be up to 64K bytes in size, this sequential version of the Z8000 can address up to 8 megabytes of memory. The sequential version of the Z8000 also has a segment trap control input ($\overline{SEGT}$). This input is much like an interrupt input, designed to trap specific processor operations.

		Control bus		
		Inputs	Outputs	
Address	*Data*	*Inputs*	*Outputs*	*Power supply*
16 bits in 40-pin	16 bits,	$\overline{\text{WAIT}}$	ST0-ST3	5 V
version multiplexed	bidirectional	$\overline{\text{STOP}}$	$\overline{\text{AS}}$	
on data bus		$\overline{\text{BUSRQ}}$	$\overline{\text{DS}}$	
23 bits in		$\overline{\text{NMI}}$	$\overline{\text{MREQ}}$	
48-pin version		$\overline{\text{VI}}$	$\overline{\text{READ/WRITE}}$	
		$\overline{\text{NVI}}$	$\overline{\text{NORMAL/SYSTEM}}$	
		$\overline{\mu\text{I}}$	$\overline{\text{WORD/BYTE}}$	
		$\overline{\text{SEGT}}$	$\overline{\text{BUSAK}}$	
		$\overline{\text{RESET}}$	μ0	
		CLK		

FIGURE 3–16
Summary of Z8000 pinout.

The Z8000 requires a single 5-V power supply and a single 5-V clock input and has an active low reset line. A summary of the Z8000 pinout is given in Fig. 3-16. The Z8000 is a 16-bit processor that evolved from the 8-bit Z80, and yet has 5 to 10 times the throughput of the Z80.

TABLE 3-2
Performance Comparison of Representative Microprocessors over a 10-year Evolution*

	8008	8080	Z80	8748	8086	Z8000
Year introduced	1972	1973	1976	1977	1978	1979
Data path width (bits)	8	8	8	8	16	16
Directly addressable memory space (bytes)	16K	64K	64K	4K	1024K	8192K
Power supply voltage required (volts)	+5 −9	+12 + 5 − 5	+5	+5	+5	+5
Resident program memory	None	None	None	1K	None	None
Estimated relative throughput (8008 = 1)	1	10	20	20	100	100

*The design of the 8008 began in 1969 and the Z8000 was introduced in 1979.

SUMMARY

The evolution of microprocessors has taken place in a sequence of generations. Each successive generation has produced microprocessors with more capability in terms of speed, power of the instruction set, and ease of use. Table 3-2 compares representative microprocessors over the first 10 years of microprocessor development. During this decade of development, the overall performance or throughput of microprocessors has increased a hundredfold.

EXERCISES

3-1   How is address information output with the 8008 microprocessor?

3-2   Which line of the 8080 indicates the state of the interrupt enable flip-flop?

3-3   What signal of the 8080 is used to indicate that status information is available on the data bus?

3-4   What are the differences distinguishing the hold, wait, and halt states of the 8080 microprocessor?

3-5   What control line of the Z80 microprocessor is used to initiate a DMA operation?

3-6   What is the difference between the INT and the NMI inputs of the Z80 microprocessor?

3-7   What is the purpose of the ALE output of the 8748?

3-8   How many words of memory space can be directly addressed by each of these microprocessors:

a. 8008   b. 8080   c. Z80   d. 8748   e. Z8000
f. 8086.

3-9   What technology is used in the manufacturing of each of these microprocessors:

a. 8008   b. 8080   c. Z80   d. 8748   e. Z8000
f. 8086.

3-10 Select a microprocessor *not* discussed in this chapter and list its: (a) power supply requirements, (b) data bus size, (c) address bus size, (d) control bus lines (by function).

REFERENCES

8008 Microprocessor Intel 8008 8-Bit Parallel Central Processor Unit User's Manual, 1973.

8080 Microprocessor Intel 8080 Microcomputer Systems User's Manual, 1975.

Z80 Microprocessor Zilog Z80 CPU Technical Manual, 1976.

8748 Microprocessor Intel MCS-48 Microcomputer User's Manual, 1978.

8086 Microprocessor Intel MCS-86 Product Description, 1978.

Z8000 Microprocessor Zilog Z8000 CPU Technical Manual, 1979.

BASIC MICROPROCESSOR HARDWARE

Microprocessors do require some basic support circuitry when used in system design. Power-supply circuitry, for example, is needed to deliver proper supply voltages at adequate current levels to both the microprocessor and its associated circuitry. Clock circuitry may be required to generate proper timing signals. External memory is required for most microprocessors together with the memory interface circuitry. And additional logic circuitry and signal buffers are required when interfacing with input and output devices.

In this chapter the basic support circuitry required in microprocessor design is described in detail. Detailed circuit diagrams are given, complete with parts values. The chapter concludes by showing how various elements of support circuitry can be connected to a microprocessor to obtain a complete, working microprocessor system.

POWER SUPPLY

Microprocessors require one or more power-supply voltages. These voltages normally must be held within 5 percent of their nominal value. Microprocessor power-supply design is greatly simplified by making use of three-terminal IC voltage regulators such as the 78xx series (for positive voltages) and the 79xx series (for negative voltages). Circuit diagrams for both a positive and a negative supply using these regulators is shown in Fig. 4-1. In each case, the value of the capacitor C must be sufficiently large to assure that there is at least a 3-V differential between V_{in} and V_{out}, even during the ripple valley of the power-supply voltage. Typically, a capacitance of several thousand microfarads is used.

In designing with three-terminal IC regulators, attention must be given to the power dissipation capabilities of the regulators. Such a regulator can

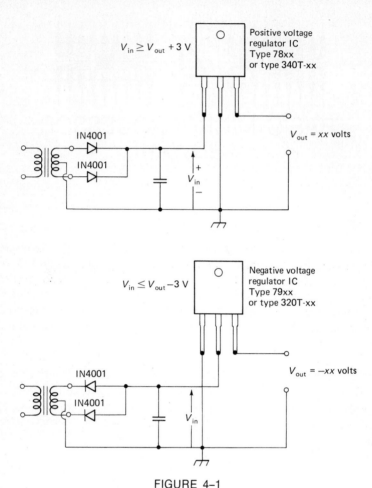

FIGURE 4-1
The use of positive and negative voltage regulator ICs for
regulated power-supply circuits.

typically dissipate 1 to 2 W of power, depending on the adequacy of the
heat sink to which it is mechanically attached. The power dissipation in the
regulator can be calculated from

$$P_{\text{diss}} = (V_{\text{out}} - V_{\text{in}}) \cdot I_{\text{load}}$$

where the power dissipation is in watts, voltages are measured in volts, and
load current is in amperes.

Some microprocessors, such as the 8080, require more than one supply
voltage. In such cases, separate regulators can be used for each voltage
required, as shown in Fig. 4-2. Some microprocessors can be operated

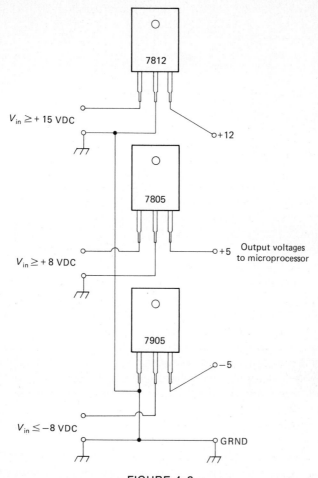

FIGURE 4–2
A triple-output power supply suitable for use with the
8080 microprocessor.

directly from batteries without the need for a voltage-regulated supply. CMOS and I²L microprocessors (see Chap. 2) are particularly well-suited to battery operation. These microprocessors generally require low supply current and are tolerant of large voltage variations.

CLOCK

The clock signals in a microprocessor system are timing waveforms that are used to synchronize the system's operation. Some microprocessors

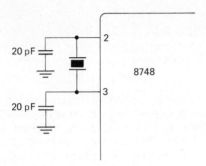

FIGURE 4–3
The 8748 family of microprocessors requires only three passive
components for the clock circuitry.

have an internal oscillator to generate a clock signal; these microprocessors require only external, passive timing components. Other microprocessors do not have an internal oscillator, and require more complicated
external circuitry to generate the clock waveforms.

The 8748 family of microprocessors is an example of a class of
microprocessors with internal oscillators. As seen in Fig. 4-3, a quartz
crystal and two capacitors are connected externally. The crystal can range
from 1 to 6 MHz, depending on the desired speed of operation. The clock
signal itself is generated internally within the microprocessor.

The Z80 microprocessor requires an externally-generated clock signal

FIGURE 4–4
A single-phase-clock generation circuit suitable for the Z80 and
other microprocessors. Output frequency is determined by the
crystal.

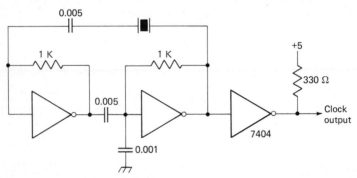

swinging from 0 to 5 V. The frequency of this signal can range from 500 kHz to 4 MHz. The schematic diagram of a circuit that can be used to generate this clock waveform is shown in Fig. 4-4.

The 8080 is an example of a microprocessor that uses two externally-

FIGURE 4–5

(*a*) Timing requirements for the Ø1 and Ø2 clock waveforms for the 8080 microprocessor. (*b*) The clock generator circuitry for the 8080 can be greatly simplified by using the 8224 clock generator IC.

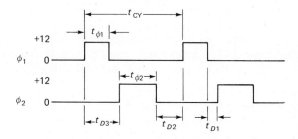

		Minimum	Maximum	
t_{CY}	Clock period	0.48	2.0	μs
$t_{\phi 1}$	Ø1 pulse width	60		ns
$t_{\phi 2}$	Ø2 pulse width	220		ns
t_{D1}	Delay Ø1 to Ø2	0		ns
t_{D2}	Delay Ø2 to Ø1	70		ns
t_{D3}	Delay Ø1 to Ø2 (lead)	130		ns
t_r, t_g	Clock rise and fall	5	50	ns

(*a*)

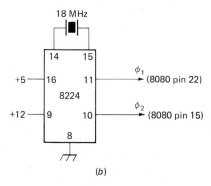

(*b*)

generated clock signals, $\emptyset 1$ and $\emptyset 2$. These clock signals swing between 0 and 12 V and must be nonoverlapping. The detailed timing relationship between these two waveforms is shown in Fig. 4-5a. A special integrated circuit, the 8224, is designed for the express function of generating the clock signals for the 8080. A schematic diagram of the 8224 used in this way is shown in Fig. 4-5b.

LOGIC GATES

Logic gates are used in microprocessor systems for control-signal decoding and for address decoding. The Z80 microprocessor, for example, uses the $\overline{M1}$ and $\overline{IORQ}$ control lines to indicate that it is responding to an interrupt. When both of these signals go to logic 0, the microprocessor is acknowledging the interrupt. In order to generate an active-high interrupt acknowledge signal (INTA) from the signals available on the Z80 control bus, a NOR gate is used as shown in Fig. 4-6. INTA is at logic 1 only when both $\overline{M1}$ and $\overline{IORQ}$ are at logic 0.

The TTL (transistor-transistor logic) family of logic gates is most commonly used to interface with microprocessors. Within the TTL family there are high-speed, high-powered parts (H series); fast, Schottky-clamped parts (S series); low-powered Schottky parts (LS series); slower, low-powered parts (L series); as well as standard TTL parts. A 7402 TTL IC, for example, containing four NOR gates in a single 14-pin package (Fig. 4-7) is available as a 7402 (standard TTL), a 74H02 (high-speed, high-power), a 74S02 (Schottky-clamped), a 74LS02 (low-powered Schottky), or as a 74L02 (slow, low-powered).

The table in Fig. 4-8 summarizes the electrical characteristics of each of the five series of TTL logic gates. This table gives the average power consumption per gate, the output drive capability of each gate at logic 0 (I_{OL}), the current required at each gate input at logic 0 (I_{IL}), and the typical propagation delay of the gate in nanoseconds. While the TTL family of logic gates is the one most commonly used with microprocessors, the CMOS

FIGURE 4–6
A 74LSO2 NOR gate is used to decode the interrupt acknowl-edge control signal from the Z80 control bus.

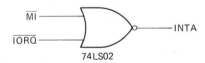

Dip (top view)

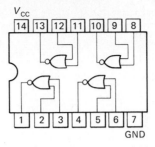

FIGURE 4–7
The 7402 TTL IC contains
four NOR gates in a sin-
gle 14-pin dual in-line
package (DIP).

family of logic gates is used when low-powered operation is more
important than high-speed operation (e.g., in battery-powered applications). The electrical characteristics of the CMOS family are also summarized in the table of Fig. 4-8.

Example

An output of the Z80 microprocessor is used to drive several low-power
Schottky gate inputs. A Z80 output is able to sink 1.8 mA of current when it

FIGURE 4–8
Electrical characteristics of various logic families used to interface with
microprocessors.

Logic family	Power dissipation per gate, mW	Input current required, I_{IL}, μA	Output current available, I_{OL}, mA	Typical propagation delay, t_P, ns
TTL 74S	19	2000	20	3
TTL 74H	22	2000	20	6
TTL 74	10	1600	16	10
TTL 74LS	2	400	8	10
TTL 74L	1	180	3.6	33
CMOS	0.001	0.00001	0.6	35

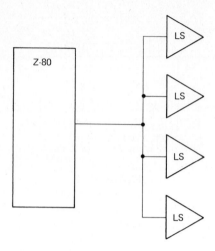

FIGURE 4–9
The Z80 microprocessor can drive
four 74LS TTL loads without additional buffering.

is at logic 0. How many gate inputs can be directly driven by the microprocessor?

Answer   From the table of Fig. 4-8 we see that each low-power Schottky gate input requires a maximum current sink of 0.4 mA in the logic 0 state. Thus the Z80 can drive four LS TTL gates directly (Fig. 4-9). The current required by TTL inputs in the logic 1 state is small, and is seldom a design constraint as long as the logic 1 voltage requirement is met.

The example shown in Fig. 4-6 demonstrated how a 74LS02 NOR gate could be used in control-signal decoding. Another important use of logic gates in microprocessor systems is in *address decoding*. Suppose, for example, that a microprocessor system has one 4K block of memory residing from address E000 to EFFF in memory space. Logic gates can be used to detect when the address on the microprocessor address bus is in this range, and generate a valid address (VA) signal to enable this block of memory. A circuit that can be used to carry out this address decoding uses one inverter and one 4-input AND gate, as shown in Fig. 4-10.

As another example of address decoding, suppose a circuit is needed to allow a user to position a 4K block of memory at various addresses in memory space by using four switches to set the high-order hexadecimal digit of the address. A circuit to do this using just one IC is shown in Fig. 4-11. Here, a 74LS136 quad exclusive-OR gate with open-collector outputs

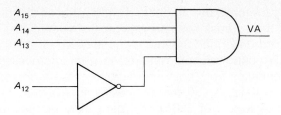

FIGURE 4–10
Address decoding circuit. Valid Address signal
is generated for addresses in the range of
E000 to EFFF.

FIGURE 4–11
A single 74LS136 is used to decode
the high-order nybble of the microprocessor address bus.

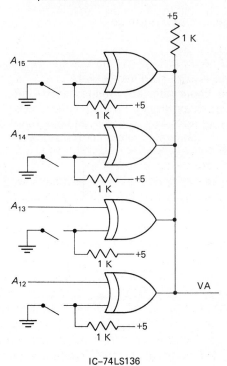

IC–74LS136

is used. If the switches are all open, a valid address signal is generated only when all the address lines are at logic 0. This circuit is one used in a 4K memory card described in more detail in Chap. 5.

Many of the control signals required in a microprocessor system are based on information from both the microprocessor address bus and the control bus (Fig. 4-12). A Z80 microprocessor, for example, can output data on the data bus to any of 256 output ports. The fact that output data is available is signaled by both $\overline{WR}$ and $\overline{IORQ}$ going to logic 0. The port address (to select one of 256 ports) is given by the eight address lines A0 through A7. The circuit diagram of Fig. 4-13 shows how logic gates can be used to generate an output strobe signal to a specific port. In this example, the output port address is FF.

LATCHES

Very often in microprocessor systems, information may appear on a microprocessor bus that must be retained for subsequent system use. Information sent to an output port, for example, may need to be retained for some period of time after the information was actually transferred on the microprocessor data bus. In situations like this, a *latch* can be used to save the required data.

FIGURE 4–12
Logic gates are used to decode information from both the microprocessor
control bus and the address bus to
generate system-control signals.

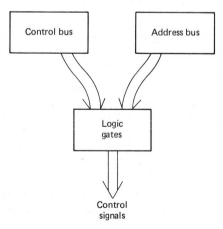

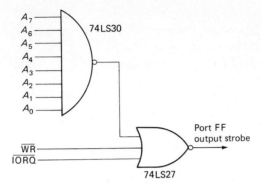

FIGURE 4–13

Logic gates are used to decode the address bus and control bus in a Z80 system to generate an output strobe signal to port FF.

Systems using an 8080 microprocessor require a *status latch* to retain the status information that the 8080 multiplexes on the data bus at the beginning of every machine cycle. When the $\phi1$ clock and the SYNC control line are both at logic 1, there is new status information on the data bus. An 8212 latch (Fig. 4-14) can be used to latch this status information as shown in Fig. 4-15.

The 8212 8-bit latch can also be used as part of a microprocessor *output port*. Logic gates are used to detect when data is output to a specific port (as in Fig. 4-13) and to generate a strobe signal to activate the output latch. The complete schematic diagram of an output port is shown in Fig. 4-16.

Yet another example of how latches are used in microprocessor systems is for the purpose of *address latching*. The 8748 microprocessor, for example, multiplexes the eight low-order bits of address information on the data bus at the beginning of a machine cycle. Again, an 8212 8-bit latch can be used to retain this address information for subsequent use in the machine cycle. A special line of the 8748 control bus, address latch enable (ALE), is used to activate the 8212. Fig. 4-17 shows the schematic diagram of an 8748 with its address latch.

BUFFERS

A *buffer* is an amplifier that can be used to increase the current drive capability of a microprocessor signal line. Buffers with tristate outputs can

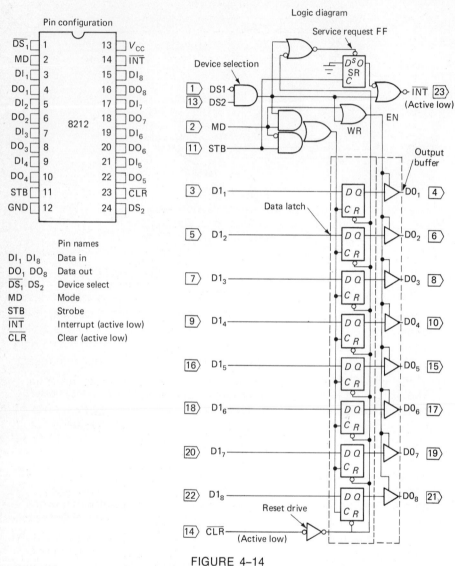

FIGURE 4–14

The 8212 IC can be used as an 8-bit latch when the MD input is at logic 1 or as an 8-bit buffer when the MD input is at logic 0.

also be used to provide electrical isolation between portions of a microprocessor system.

One important use of a buffer is in a microprocessor *input port*. In this use, the buffer serves to isolate input data from the microprocessor data bus until input data is requested by the microprocessor. Logic gates can

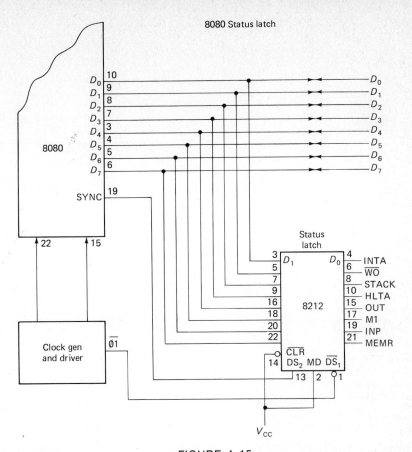

FIGURE 4–15
The 8212 is used to latch the status information on the data bus at the
coincidence of Ø1 and SYNC.

FIGURE 4–16
Output port at address FF.

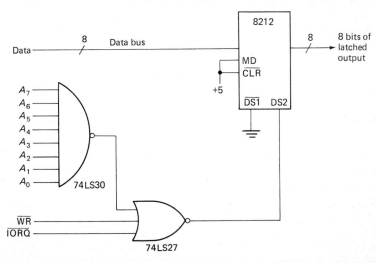

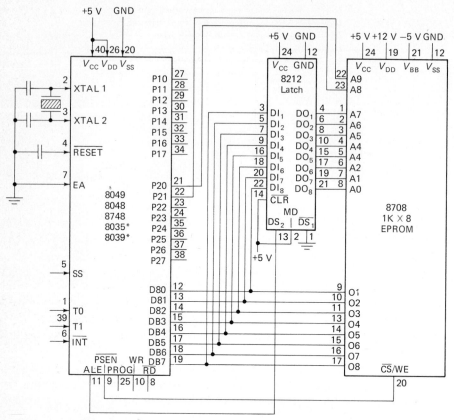

*EA = 5 V FOR 8035/8039

FIGURE 4–17

An 8212 is used as an address latch when interfacing the 2708 memory chip to the 8748 microprocessor. *Note:* the 8212 serves as an address latch. Address is valid while ALE is high and is latched when ALE goes low.

be used to detect a request for input data from a specific input port and to generate the input strobe signal. For the Z80 microprocessor, the $\overline{\text{IORQ}}$ signal and the $\overline{\text{RD}}$ signal go to logic 0 to indicate an input request. When these two lines are at logic 0, the address of the selected input port is on the eight low-order bits of the address bus. Figure 4-18 shows an 8212 used as an 8-bit buffer in an input port circuit. Note that the mode pin of the 8212 (MD) is set at a logic 0 level in order that the 8212 can be used as a tristate buffer. In this circuit example, the address decoding is designed to detect input port address FF.

Bidirectional microprocessor lines can be buffered with *bidirectional drivers*. As shown in Fig. 4-19, a bidirectional driver can be formed from

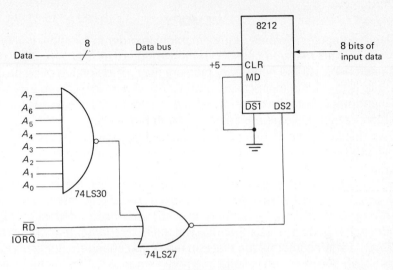

FIGURE 4–18
Input port at address FF.

two tristate buffers connected head-to-tail with an inverter between the two tristate enable lines to assure that only one of the buffers is enabled at any one time. Bidirectional drivers are available in standard IC packages (e.g. the 8216).

FIGURE 4–19
Two tristate buffers and an inverter can be used to form a bidirectional buffer. The control signal determines which amplifier is active.

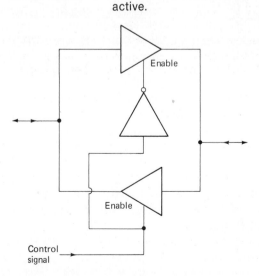

MEMORY

All microcomputer systems require memory in order to function. It is in this memory that the microprocessor program is stored, as is any required data. In some cases, all the necessary memory may reside on the microprocessor chip itself. But in most cases, additional memory is required external to the microprocessor. The types of semiconductor memory now available for microprocessor systems are summarized in Fig. 4-20.

Two distinct types of memory may be used in a microprocessor system: (1) volatile memory or (2) nonvolatile memory. Volatile memory has the characteristic that once power is removed from it, the information that was stored in the memory is lost. By contrast, the contents of nonvolatile memory are not lost when power is removed. *Read-only memory* (ROM) is an example of nonvolatile memory that contains fixed information that is either unchangeable or changeable with difficulty. *Random-access memory* (RAM) contains information that can readily be changed. Semiconductor RAM is an example of volatile memory. Magnetic core memory is an example of nonvolatile RAM.

Referring again to Fig. 4-20, a ROM can be classified as either factory-programmed or user-programmed. Factory programmed ROM is given a set memory pattern at the time of manufacture as determined by the IC metallization mask. These mask-programmed ROMs are very reliable and, when produced in volume, provide the lowest cost per bit of any semiconductor memory. User programmable ROM, or PROM, can be of two types. Fuse-link PROMs can be programmed just once, after which the pattern cannot be changed. Erasable PROMs (EPROM) can be erased by the user and reprogrammed. There are now two varieties of erasable PROM. One variety, called UV EPROM, is erased by shining an intense ultraviolet light on the IC itself. The UV EPROM is very popular for microprocessor prototyping work. A photograph of the 2716 UV EPROM, which has a 2K-byte memory capacity, is shown in Fig. 4-21. The other variety of

FIGURE 4–20
Summary of available semiconductor memories for microprocessor systems.

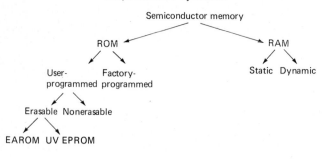

(a)

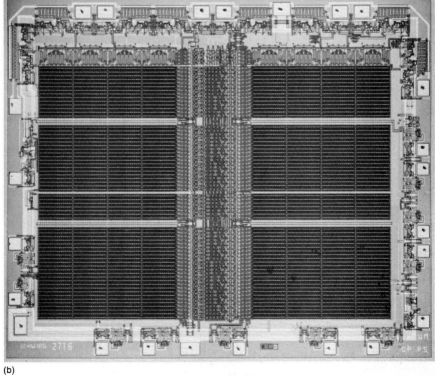

(b)

FIGURE 4–21
The 2716 UV EPROM has a 2K-byte memory capacity. (a) packaged IC. (b)
photomicrograph of IC chip (Intel Corporation)

erasable PROM is called EAROM (electrically-alterable read-only memory) and is erased electrically rather than with UV light.

RAM is classified as either *static* memory or *dynamic* memory. In dynamic memory, information is stored as charges that will dissipate if not continually refreshed. External refresh circuitry is required when using dynamic RAM. Static memory, on the other hand, requires no such refresh circuitry since the information is stored in latched flip-flops. Although dynamic memory does require external refresh circuitry, it is less expensive than static memory and consumes less power.

As an example of how a memory IC can be interfaced to a microprocessor system, consider the 2708 EPROM shown in Fig. 4-22. The 2708 has 10 address lines that are connected to the 10 low-order address lines of the microprocessor address bus. The chip select (CS) input to the 2708 is brought to logic 0 when there is a memory read operation in the address space in which the 2708 resides. If the 2708 is used in the lowest 1K of memory space in a Z80 system, the circuit required is shown in Fig. 4-23. When $\overline{RD}$, $\overline{MREQ}$, and A10 through A15 are at logic 0, the $\overline{CS}$ input of the 2708 is brought to logic 0 and a memory read takes place in the first 1K of memory space.

FIGURE 4–22
The 2708 UV EPROM.

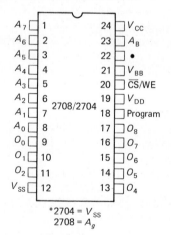

*2704 = V_{SS}
2708 = A_9

Pin names

$A_0 - A_9$	Address inputs
$O_1 - O_8$	Data outputs
$\overline{CS}$/WE	Chip select/write enable input

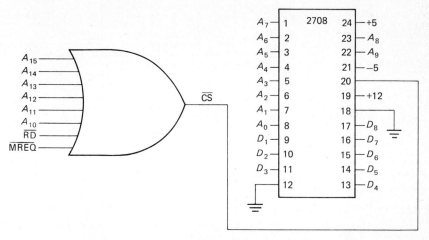

FIGURE 4–23
Interfacing the 2708 to the Z80 microprocessor.

MINIMAL MICROPROCESSOR SYSTEMS

Now, the various elements of microprocessor hardware discussed above can be combined to produce a complete, working microprocessor system. A very minimal system with one input port, one output port, and 1K of PROM will be considered. This minimal system is configured for each of three different microprocessors: the 8080, the Z80, and the 8748.

A diagram of a minimal 8080 system is shown in Fig. 4-24. Since there is only one memory chip, one input port, and one output port, address decoding is not included in this circuit. There can be no ambiguity as to which memory chip or which input or output port is being accessed in this system. Notice that the 8080 does require a status latch, three power-supply voltages, and two externally-generated clock signals.

A minimal Z80 system is shown in Fig. 4-25. The system requires one power-supply voltage and one externally-generated clock signal. All required control signals are available on the Z80 control bus, and so no status latch is required in Z80 system designs.

The 8748 microprocessor has 1-K byte of PROM on the microprocessor chip itself. It also incorporates two bidirectional I/O ports. The minimal configuration shown in Fig. 4-26 requires very little external circuitry. The 8748, then, clearly shines in small-system design. This micro-processor, however, is not as easily expanded in larger systems as is the 8080 or Z80.

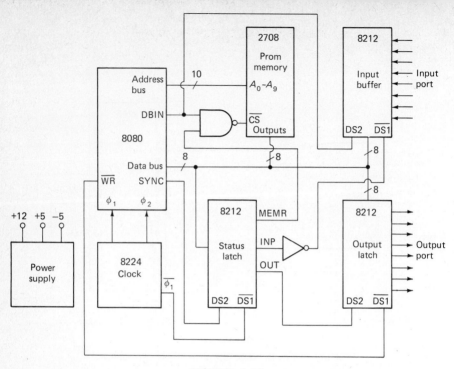

FIGURE 4-24

A complete microprocessor system using the 8080. *Note:* Since only one input port, one output port, and one memory IC are used in this system, no address decoding is required for port selection or memory chip selection.

FIGURE 4-25

A complete microprocessor system using the Z80 microprocessor. No status latch is required. The system requires a single +5-V supply and a single clock line.

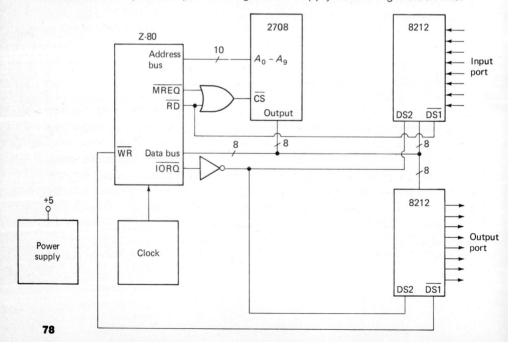

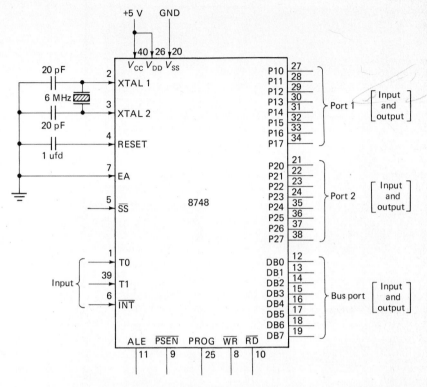

FIGURE 4–26

A complete microprocessor system using the 8748 microprocessor. *Note:* All inputs and outputs are standard TTL compatible. P1 and P2 outputs drive 5-V CMOS directly. Others require 10 to 50-kΩ pull-up. XTAL: series resonant; AT cut; 1 to 6 MHz.

SINGLE-CARD COMPUTERS

Microprocessors are commonly available on a small printed circuit board containing much of the external support circuitry that has been discussed in this chapter. In many system designs, this "single-card computer" serves as the center of the design, rather than the microprocessor itself. Beginning a design with a single-card computer frees the designer from some of the details of the microprocessor hardware design and lets the designer focus on system design problems.

An example of such a single-card computer from Cromemco is pictured in Fig. 4-27. This product uses a Z80 microprocessor operating at a 4-MHz clock rate. A 4-MHz crystal oscillator is included on the card. The card also

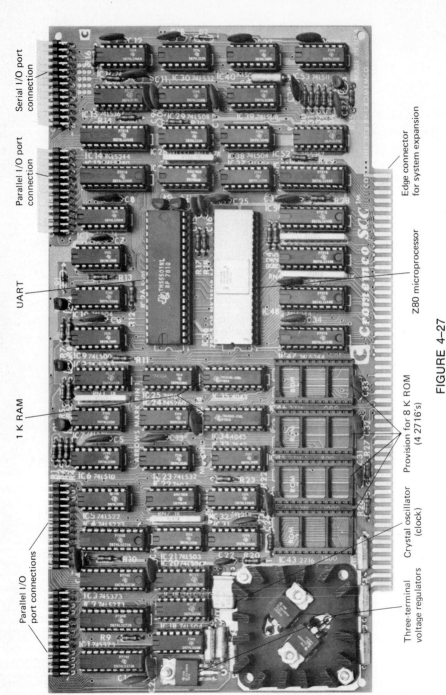

FIGURE 4–27

A single-card computer. (*Cromemco Incorporated.*)

has the capacity for 8K bytes of PROM (in 2716 PROMs) and has 1K byte of RAM. The card includes three 8-bit input ports and three 8-bit output ports as well as an RS-232 serial port (see Chap. 10).

Although single-card computers can be used in stand-alone systems, the processor data bus, address bus, and control bus are brought to edge contacts on the card. As a result, the capability of the single-card computer can be greatly expanded into a multi-card system with additional memory or I/O interface boards added as needed.

SUMMARY

A minimal microprocessor system normally requires, in addition to the microprocessor itself, a regulated power supply, clocks, logic gates, latches, buffers, and external memory. Some microprocessors, known as "single-chip computers," contain much of this support circuitry on the microprocessor IC itself. Other microprocessors require a complete complement of external support circuitry to be useful. Complete microprocessor systems are commercially available on standard printed circuit cards. These single-card computers have all the required microprocessor support circuitry already in place and can be put to immediate use.

EXERCISES

4-1   A three-terminal IC regulator (a 7805) has a maximum current rating of 1.5 A and a maximum power rating of 2 W. If 8 V is connected to the input of the regulator, what is the maximum allowable load current?

4-2   What type of logic gate should be used when low power consumption is of prime importance?

4-3   How many L series TTL inputs can be driven by one standard TTL output?

4-4   How many LS series TTL inputs can be driven by one S series TTL output?

4-5   Draw the circuit diagram of a Z80 output port at address CD.

4-6   Draw the circuit diagram of a Z80 input port at address F7.

4-7 Show a Z80 system with 1K of EPROM (a 2708) from address E400 to E7FF in memory space.

4-8 Describe the characteristics of magnetic core memories.

4-9 Describe the differences between static and dynamic memories.

4-10 Show the schematic diagram of a minimal microprocessor system for some microprocessor other than ones discussed in this chapter.

5
EXPANDING THE
MICROPROCESSOR SYSTEM

In Chap. 4, the hardware required to implement a minimal microprocessor system was discussed. In some applications, no further hardware is required. If you are to use the microprocessor to its full potential, however, much could be added to this minimal circuitry.

In particular, this chapter will discuss how to increase the memory and I/O capacity of the microprocessor. It will show how a microprocessor can be synchronized with slow memory or I/O devices, and the circuitry that allows you to "single-step" through a microprocessor program will be discussed. The use of interrupts, direct memory access, memory-mapped I/O, and address anticipation will also be discussed.

SYNCHRONIZATION OF DATA TRANSFER

Normally, a microprocessor sequences through its program at a rate set only by the microprocessor clock. It can be very useful to break this lock step to force the microprocessor to "wait" before proceeding. Such a capability is important when synchronizing a microprocessor to slower memory or I/O, or when troubleshooting a microprocessor system.

Most microprocessors have a control input line that can be used to cause the microprocessor to pause and enter a waiting state. This is the READY line of the 8080, the $\overline{WAIT}$ line of the Z80, and the $\overline{SINGLE\ STEP}$ line of the 8748. One important use of this line is in synchronizing slow memory devices to the microprocessor.

The *access time* of a memory device is defined as the latency from when the memory device is given a valid address until the outputs contain valid data. Every microprocessor system has a certain *system access time*. If the access time of the memory used with the microprocessor system is less than the system access time, then the microprocessor system can run at full speed. If, on the other hand, the memory access time is *longer* than the system access time, special provisions must be made to synchronize the slow memory devices with the system.

The system access time for the 8080 microprocessor with a 2-MHz clock frequency, for example, can be found from the manufacturer's data sheet as shown in Fig. 5-1. As seen from this timing diagram, a valid address is sent to the memory device during T1. Valid data must be available for the microprocessor 650 ns later (the system access time) during T3. If the access time of the memory is greater than 650 ns, additional circuitry must be used to extend the effective system access time.

The 8080 microprocessor interrogates its READY line during the T2 state of a machine cycle (the Z80 interrogates its $\overline{\text{WAIT}}$ line during this time). If the READY line is high, the processor proceeds directly to the T3 (data transfer) state. If the line is low, the processor enters one or more wait states until the READY line goes high, allowing the processor to proceed to the T3 state. So, the effective system access time can be increased from 650 ns to 1150 by inserting one wait state between T2 and T3 as shown in Fig. 5-2.

When memory with a slow access time is included in a system, *wait-state generation circuitry* must be included in the system design. This circuitry must detect when a slow device is accessed by the microprocessor, and proceed to hold down the READY line for the required number of wait states. The wait-state generation circuitry shown in Fig. 5-3 is designed to detect a memory read to slow memory and signal "not ready" to the microprocessor. One, two, three, or four wait states can be inserted depending on which flip-flop output is connected to the gate input. This

FIGURE 5–1
The system access time for the 8080 microprocessor is 650 ns as computed from the
manufacturer's timing diagram.

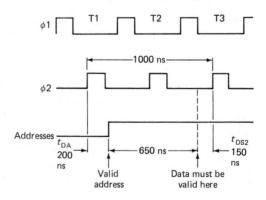

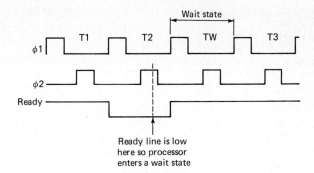

FIGURE 5–2
A logic 0 signal on the READY line can be used to
increase the system access time by an integral number of wait states.

FIGURE 5–3
Wait-state generation circuit. This circuit uses the four sections of a 74175 quad
flip-flop to form a 4-bit shift register. The SYNC pulse (which occurs at the
beginning of each machine cycle) clears the flip-flops and a 1 is then shifted
down the line. The number of shifts determines the number of wait states
inserted between T2 and T3.

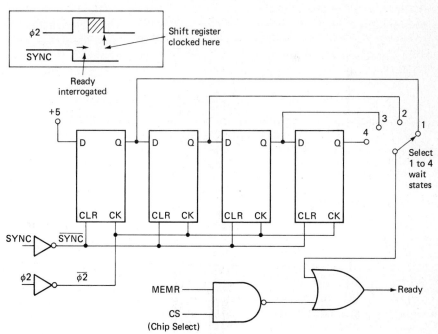

circuit uses the four sections of a 74175 quad flip-flop to form a 4-bit shift register. The SYNC pulse (which occurs at the beginning of each machine cycle) clears the flip-flops and a logic 1 is then shifted down the line. The number of shifts determines the number of wait states inserted between T2 and T3.

Another common use of the READY control line is in single-stepping through a program one machine cycle at a time. The microprocessor is made to pause during each machine cycle, thus allowing one to observe the execution of a program in minute detail. This can be particularly helpful when debugging a system. When single-stepping through a program, the READY line is held low most of the time, and is brought to a logic 1 state only when proceeding to the subsequent machine cycle. A single-step circuit that can be used with either the 8080 or 8748 microprocessor is shown in Fig. 5-4.

This circuit uses two 2-input NAND gates to debounce a push button switch. The debounced output is used to clock a D flip-flop. The flip-flop is cleared at the beginning of each machine cycle by the SYNC signal for the 8080, or by the ALE signal for the 8748. The output of the flip-flop is connected to the READY line of the 8080 or the SINGLE STEP line of the 8748.

Use of the READY line is just one technique that may be used to synchronize the flow of data in a microprocessor system. The main disadvantage of using the READY line for system synchronization is that no processing can be done while the processor is in a waiting state. If a long waiting state is required to synchronize a microprocessor to a slow peripheral device (say several hundred microseconds or longer), then the

FIGURE 5-4
Single-step circuit that can be used with either the 8080 or
8748 microprocessor.

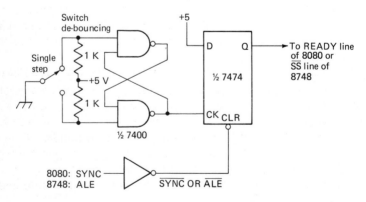

processor is losing time that could be used for the execution of other parts of the program. The operation of the microprocessor is completely limited by the peripheral device during I/O operations.

The technique of interrupt generation, on the other hand, permits the processor to operate at full speed, and service a peripheral (by sending or receiving data) only when an interrupt is generated by the peripheral. The interrupt causes the microprocessor to branch to a *restart location* in memory space, where the *interrupt service routine* resides. The interrupt service routine services the peripheral and then returns the microprocessor to the main program.

A third technique that can be used in synchronizing a microprocessor system to slow peripherals is that of system *polling*. With this technique, the microprocessor periodically inputs *status information* from one or more peripheral devices to determine whether or not it is ready to send or receive data. When a device is ready, the microprocessor branches to the appropriate data transfer routine.

INTERRUPTS

The interrupt lines in a microprocessor control bus allow an external device to interrupt the flow of a microprocessor program, forcing the program to branch to a specific location in memory. Interrupts may be *maskable* or *nonmaskable*. A maskable interrupt has the characteristic that should the microprocessor execute a disable interrupt (DI) instruction, any control signal on the interrupt line will be ignored, or masked out. The processor will remain oblivious to the masked interrupt line until an enable interrupt (EI) instruction is executed. A nonmaskable interrupt, on the other hand, cannot be masked out under program control.

Interrupts are also said to be either *vectored* or *fixed location* interrupts. A fixed location interrupt will always cause the processor to branch to one specific, unchangeable location in memory. Vectored interrupts, on the other hand, may cause a branch to any of a number of different locations depending on the signals at an *interrupt port* that is interrogated by the processor following an interrupt.

The Z80 is an example of a microprocessor with a particularly rich interrupt structure. There are two interrupt control lines, one maskable and one not. The nonmaskable interrupt (NMI) cannot be vectored. An NMI causes a branch to location 0066H in memory where the interrupt service routine must begin. The interrupt service routine is terminated by a return instruction which forces the microprocessor to return to exactly where it was in the main program at the time of the interrupt.

The Z80 may respond in one of three ways to its maskable interrupt, depending on which of three interrupt modes has been selected by the microprocessor program. Mode 1 is a nonvectored interrupt mode. An interrupt on the maskable interrupt line while the processor is in this mode causes a branch to the fixed memory location 0038H. Mode 0 is a vectored interrupt mode that is identical to the interrupt mode used in the 8080 microprocessor. A mode 0 interrupt forces the processor to fetch its next executable instruction not from memory, but from the interrupt port. The circuit shown in Fig. 4-6 can be used to detect an interrogation of the interrupt port (interrupt acknowledge) and strobe the next executable instruction onto the data bus. The complete circuit diagram of an interrupt port is shown in Fig. 5-5. Although the interrupt port can apply any instruction to the data bus, the restart instruction is the one most commonly used. The restart instruction, discussed in more detail in the next chapter, is able to vector the processor to any one of eight restart locations in memory.

Mode 2 is also a vectored interrupt mode. In this mode, the address of the interrupt service routine is stored in two bytes of memory space (since it is a 16-bit vector). During the interrupt acknowledge cycle, the processor determines the address of this vector from its own internal 8-bit I register and from the interrupt port. The eight high-order bits of the vector address are given by the I register and the eight low-order bits are given by the interrupt port, where the least-significant bit is assumed to be 0.

SERIAL DATA TRANSMISSION

In the discussion of input ports and output ports in Chap. 4, it was assumed that devices communicating with an 8-bit microprocessor always accom-

FIGURE 5–5
Interrupt port.

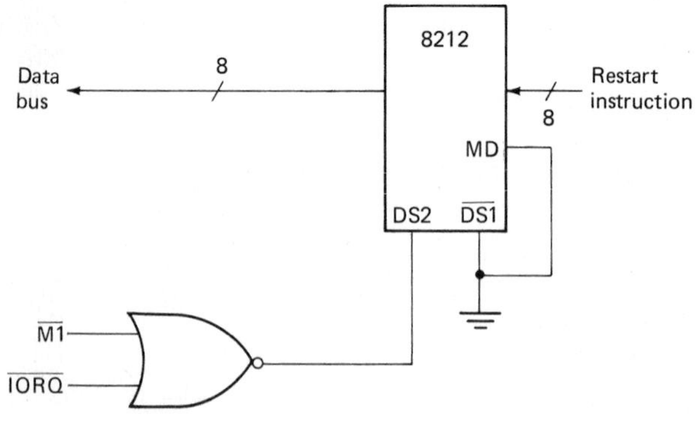

modate 8-bits of data in parallel. In fact, however, many common peripherals to microprocessor systems do not have this capability. Such peripherals, instead, are designed to send and receive data *serially* in time over a single transmission line. Common peripherals that use serial data include teletypes, CRT terminals, and modems.

One of two approaches may be taken when using a microprocessor with serial data. One approach is simply to use just 1 bit of an 8-bit port for the serial data stream, relying on the microprocessor program for the encoding and decoding of the serial data. This approach is known colloquially as "bit-banging."

A second and more common approach is to use a special hardware device for the conversion between parallel and serial data. Such a device is called a *UART* (universal asynchronous receiver transmitter). Most UARTs are available in a 40-pin IC package, as shown on the single-card computer of Fig. 4-27.

The application of the UART is shown diagrammatically in Fig. 5-6. Although the UART itself is a single IC, it can be thought of as a separate receiver (to convert serial data to 8-bit parallel data) and transmitter (to convert 8-bit parallel data to serial). The rate of transmission of serial data, in bits per second, is called the *baud rate* and is set up by an external clock signal applied to the UART. Separate clocks can be used for the receiver and the transmitter.

FIGURE 5-6
Block diagram of a UART.

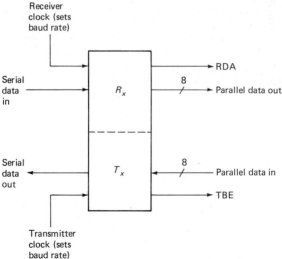

There are two important control signals available from the UART. One of these control signals is *receiver data available*, or RDA, and is used to indicate that a complete 8-bit word of serial data has been received. The second signal is *transmitter buffer empty*, or TBE. The TBE signal is used to indicate that the UART is able to accept a new 8-bit parallel byte of data for transmission. These two signals must be used by the microprocessor in order to provide synchronization with the external device.

One way the microprocessor can have access to this information is by dedicating one input port to the task of polling the status of the UART. A common convention, shown in Fig. 5-7, is to use input port 0 for the status port with TBE as the most-significant bit and RDA as the next most-significant bit. Data transmission, however, occurs over I/O port 1. Another common scheme is to use RDA and TBE to activate interrupts to indicate their status.

FIGURE 5–7
Interfacing a UART to a microprocessor system.

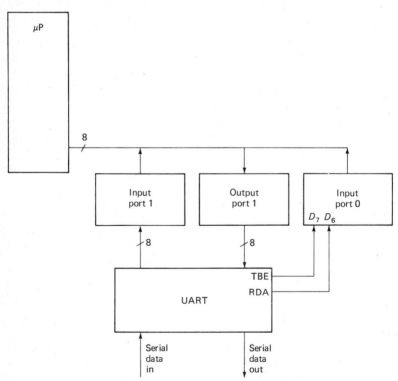

DIRECT MEMORY ACCESS

The most rapid way for an external device to read or write memory in a microprocessor system is by direct memory access (DMA). The external device must provide all address and control signals required for the proper operation of the memory. The rate of data transfer is limited only by the access time of the memory.

There are two possible modes of DMA operation. In one mode, called *visible DMA*, the operation of the microprocessor is temporarily suspended while the external device accesses the memory. The second possible mode, called *transparent DMA* or *cycle stealing*, synchronizes external access of the memory with the processor's access of memory allowing DMA to proceed without interfering with the microprocessor operation.

The visible DMA operation commences with the external device requesting control of the address and data buses. This request is made by applying a logic 1 signal to the HOLD input of the 8080 or a logic 0 signal to the BUSRQ input of the Z80. At the end of the next machine cycle, the microprocessor suspends operation and acknowledges that it has re-

FIGURE 5–8
DMA circuitry.

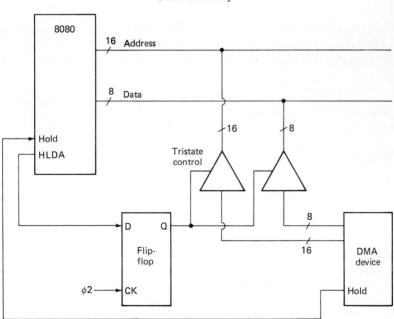

sponded to the hold request. The 8080 responds with a HLDA (hold acknowledge) signal, and the Z80 responds with a $\overline{\text{BUSAK}}$ signal. After an appropriate delay following the acknowledge signal (as found from the manufacturer's data sheet), the external device can take control of the microprocessor buses: the microprocessor outputs are in the high-impedance state (tristate). Figure 5-8 shows the circuitry that can be used with a DMA device and an 8080 microprocessor. On the falling edge of $\phi2$ following HLDA, the flip-flop clocks through the HLDA signal to activate the tristate buffers of the DMA device.

A transparent DMA operation can occur only if the DMA device is synchronized never to access a specific block of memory at the same time the processor needs access to the memory. One approach, called cycle stealing, is to access memory only when the processor is engaged in some other activity, such as instruction decoding. Another approach uses a *two-port memory* architecture with the processor accessing memory through one port and the DMA device accessing memory through another port. As long as the DMA device does not access the same block of memory at the same time as the processor, the device can have free access to all other blocks of memory.

MEMORY-MAPPED I/O

Microprocessors such as the 8080 and Z80 can address 256 output ports and 256 input ports by use of output and input instructions in the microprocessor program. One way to expand beyond this number of ports

FIGURE 5–9
Memory-mapped I/O can be used as shown for the output port that is at memory location FFF0H.

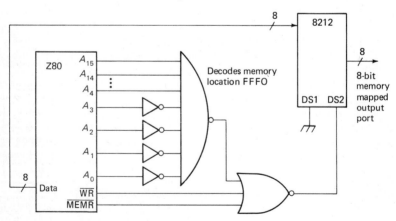

Bank select   Address select

FIGURE 5–10
RAM card with 4K-byte capacity. (*Cromemco Incorporated.*)

is to define memory locations as I/O ports. An instruction to write memory at such a location is interpreted by the external hardware as an output. An instruction to read memory is interpreted as an input. Defining I/O ports in this way is called *memory-mapped I/O*. In fact, some microprocessors, such as the 6800, have no separate input and output instructions. They use memory-mapped I/O as a matter of course. Figure 5-9 shows how a specific memory location (FFF0H) can be used as an I/O port with the Z80 microprocessor. Here, $\overline{MREQ}$ is used instead of $\overline{IORQ}$ for port selection.

MEMORY BANK SELECT

A microprocessor with 16 address lines is able to directly address 2^{16} memory (or memory-mapped I/O) locations. To expand beyond these 64K locations, a number of different schemes may be used. One of these is *memory bank select*.

With memory bank select, memory space is arranged in a number of separate banks of up to 64K each. An output instruction can be used to select the active bank.

Figure 5-10 is a 4K memory card designed for a microprocessor system that incorporates bank select. (A schematic diagram of the card is shown in Fig. 5-11.) An eight-position switch (see figure) is used to select

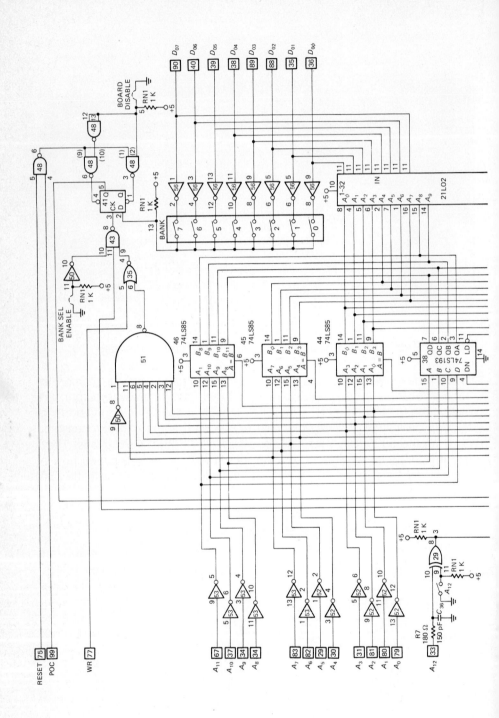

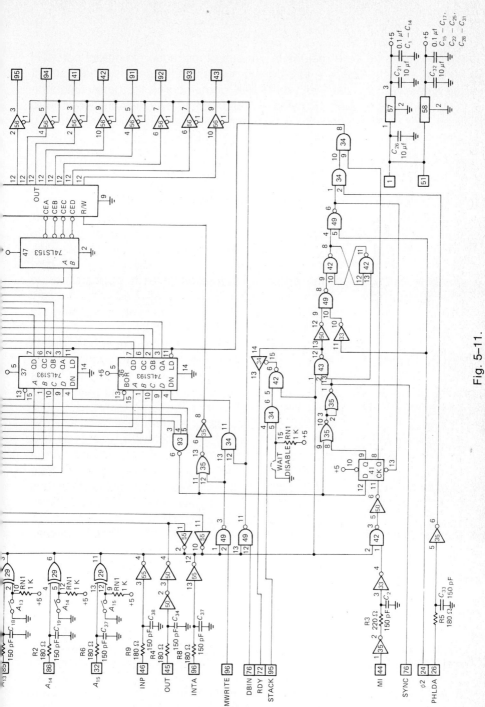

Fig. 5-11.

Schematic diagram of the memory card shown in Fig. 5-10.

which banks the card resides in. An output instruction to output port 40H selects the active bank. A four-position switch on the card is used to select the location of the card within the 64K of memory in the bank. Since the memory card contains 4K bytes of memory, four switches are required to select one of 16 positions in the 64K memory space. The address decoding circuit to do this is similar to that of Fig. 4-11.

ADDRESS ANTICIPATION

Address anticipation is a technique that can be used to increase the speed of operation of a microprocessor system. The technique of address anticipation is based on the premise that, in a microprocessor program, the addresses that appear on the address bus are very often sequential. Circuitry can thus be devised that *anticipates* the address of the next machine cycle *before* the address information actually appears on the address bus. This address information can then be applied to the memory chips much sooner than it could be otherwise, effectively increasing the system access time when the addresses are sequential.

If subsequent addresses are *not* sequential, circuitry is needed to detect this condition and insert wait states. When addresses are sequential (as they are most of the time), however, addresses may be applied for a sufficiently long time to the memory to avoid any need for wait states at all.

Figure 5-11 is a circuit diagram of a memory card, known as a 4KZ, designed for a Z80 or 8080 microprocessor system that uses address anticipation. The memory chips used are type 21L02 having an access time of 450 ns. The memory card is designed to operate in a system with a machine state time of 250 ns (4-MHz clock), and inserts a single wait state only for nonsequential addresses. The current address on the address bus is compared with the anticipated address by the 74LS85 digital comparators (IC44 to IC46). If these two addresses are equal, pin 6 of IC43 goes low to permit the memory cycle to proceed without a wait state. If the addresses are not equal, pin 6 of IC43 goes high, causing one wait state to be inserted in the cycle. Address anticipation is performed by the 74LS193 counters (IC36 to IC38). Since the address lines to this card are inverted by buffers (IC52, IC53), the 74LS193 counters actually count *down* rather than up to obtain the next sequential address in memory.

Another form of address anticipation is carried out internally in the 8086 microprocessor. The 8086 anticipates that the next six instructions to be executed follow sequentially in memory. These six instructions are stored in a queue internal to the microprocessor. The queue is filled by memory accesses that take place at the same time the processor is internally decoding or executing the current instruction. Assuming that the current instruction is not a branch instruction, the next instruction is immediately available from the queue upon completion of the current instruction without the need for a delaying memory access. If the current instruction is a branch instruction, then the queue is reset and an additional memory access is made to fetch the next instruction.

SUMMARY

Circuitry that may be used to expand the minimal microprocessor system has been discussed. As peripheral devices are added to the system, they may be synchronized by means of a system "ready" line, interrupts, or polling. A UART may be used to send or receive serial data with a microprocessor system. Direct memory access is used for the fastest possible transfer of information to or from a microprocessor system, and address anticipation may be used to minimize the retarding effect of memory access time on system performance. I/O channels may be expanded into memory space by use of memory-mapped I/O and memory space may itself be expanded through memory bank switching.

The microprocessor circuitry that has been discussed is known collectively as the system *hardware*. The operation of this hardware is governed strictly by the stored program or *software* of the system. The nature of this software and the way microprocessor programs are written are discussed in the next two chapters.

EXERCISES

5-1   Define "memory access time."

5-2   Define "system access time."

5-3   What is the main advantage of interrupt synchronization of a microprocessor peripheral over status polling?

5-4   What is a maskable interrupt?

5-5   What is a vectored interrupt?

5-6   How can a two-port memory architecture be used to effect a transparent DMA?

5-7   Draw the schematic diagram of a memory-mapped input port at address E3FF.

5-8   If each bit of a serial data stream is 1.7 ms in duration, what is the baud rate?

5-9   Referring to the schematic of Fig. 5-11, what address range in memory space is occupied by this circuit card if switches A12 and A13 are open and switches A14 and A15 are closed?

5-10   What is the purpose of address anticipation?

MICROPROCESSOR
MACHINE LANGUAGE

As stated in Chap. 1, the microprocessor operates under the control of a *program*, and the program consists of a set of *instructions*. These instructions are stored as a sequence of logic 1s and 0s in memory, and make up the *machine language* of the microprocessor.

Different microprocessors have different sets of instructions available for composing the program. The instructions of the 8748 microprocessor, for example, are different (though not radically so) from those of the 8080 microprocessor. The instruction set of the Z80 includes all the instructions of the 8080, but contains several more as well.

When working with a microprocessor, it is important to understand its instruction set and to be able to *use* these instructions in the composition of a program. It is important to understand the detailed execution of these instructions by the microprocessor and to understand how the instructions can be used to manipulate data in a microprocessor system. All these points are discussed in this chapter. Specific examples are drawn from the machine language instructions common to the 8080, 8085, and Z80 microprocessors.

BINARY REPRESENTATION OF DATA

Machine language instructions are designed to input data to the microprocessor, manipulate data within the microprocessor, and output data from the microprocessor system. There are several different ways that data may be represented using the binary code of the microprocessor. We will discuss the five most common representations used with microprocessors: (1) straight binary, (2) signed binary, (3) twos complement, (4) BCD, and (5) ASCII.

Straight Binary

In unsigned or *straight binary* representation, an n-bit microprocessor data word is simply used to represent the first 2^n nonnegative integers. An 8-bit data word, for example, can be used to represent the integers 0 through 255 as shown below:

Straight binary representation	Decimal numbers
0 0 0 0 0 0 0 0	0
0 0 0 0 0 0 0 1	1
0 0 0 0 0 0 1 0	2
0 0 0 0 0 0 1 1	3
0 0 0 0 0 1 0 0	4
.	.
.	.
.	.
1 1 1 1 1 1 1 1	255

Signed Binary

While straight binary notation is very common, it does not allow for the representation of both positive and negative numbers. One way this can be done is by dedicating the most-significant bit (MSB) of the binary word as the *sign bit*. The lower-order bits are then used to represent the *magnitude* of the number in straight binary. Again, assuming an 8-bit data word, signed binary goes like this:

Signed binary representation	Decimal numbers
0 1 1 1 1 1 1 1	+127
0 1 1 1 1 1 1 0	+126
0 0 0 0 0 0 0 0	0
1 0 0 0 0 0 0 0	0
1 1 1 1 1 1 1 0	−126
1 1 1 1 1 1 1 1	−127

Signed binary numbers are seldom used for two reasons. First, note that there are *two* representations for the number zero. This is generally an undesirable feature of a representation system. Second, note that the ordinary rules of addition for straight binary cannot be applied to signed binary numbers with consistent results. (Addition of binary numbers is discussed in Chap. 8.) Both drawbacks of the signed-binary representation system are corrected in the twos-complement notation system.

Twos Complement

Twos complement notation is the one most commonly used within microprocessors for performing arithmetic with *signed* numbers. In this notation, the negative of a binary number is represented as its twos complement. A complement of a number is formed simply by changing the 1s to 0s and the 0s to 1s. The twos complement of a number is formed by adding one to the complement of the number. For example, consider the number eleven.

$$0\ 0\ 0\ 0\ 1\ 0\ 1\ 1 = 11 \text{ decimal}$$

To find the twos complement, first complement the number:

$$1\ 1\ 1\ 1\ 0\ 1\ 0\ 0$$

And then add one:

$$1\ 1\ 1\ 1\ 0\ 1\ 0\ 1 = -11 \text{ decimal}$$

Using twos complement notation, an 8-bit data word can be used to represent the integers from -128 to $+127$ as follows:

Twos complement	Decimal number
0 1 1 1 1 1 1 1	127
0 1 1 1 1 1 1 0	126
0 0 0 0 0 0 0 1	1
0 0 0 0 0 0 0 0	0
1 1 1 1 1 1 1 1	-1
1 0 0 0 0 0 0 1	-127
1 0 0 0 0 0 0 0	-128

Binary-coded Decimal

Another common way to code numbers is with the binary-coded decimal or BCD system. In BCD notation, 4 bits are used to represent each digit of a

ASCII Character Codes

Decimal	Character	Decimal	Character	Decimal	Character
000	NUL (CTRL @)	043	+	086	V
001	SOH (CTRL A)	044	`	087	W
002	STX (CTRL B)	045	_	088	X
003	ETX (CTRL C)	046	.	089	Y
004	EOT (CTRL D)	047	/	090	Z
005	ENQ (CTRL E)	048	0	091	[
006	ACK (CTRL F)	049	1	092	\
007	BEL (CTRL G)	050	2	093	]
008	BS (CTRL H)	051	3	094	↑
009	HT (CTRL I)	052	4	095	__
010	LF (CTRL J)	053	5	096	'
011	VT (CTRL K)	054	6	097	a
012	FF (CTRL L)	055	7	098	b
013	CR (CTRL M)	056	8	099	c
014	SO (CTRL N)	057	9	100	d
015	SI (CTRL O)	058	:	101	e
016	DLE (CTRL P)	059	;	102	f
017	DC1 (CTRL Q)	060	<	103	g
018	DC2 (CTRL R)	061	=	104	h
019	DC3 (CTRL S)	062	>	105	i
020	DC4 (CTRL T)	063	?	106	j
021	NAK (CTRL U)	064	@	107	k
022	SYN (CTRL V)	065	A	108	l
023	ETB (CTRL W)	066	B	109	m
024	CAN (CTRL X)	067	C	110	n
025	EM (CTRL Y)	068	D	111	o

ASCII Character Codes

Decimal	Character	Decimal	Character	Decimal	Character
026	SUB (CTRL Z)	069	E	112	p
027	ESCAPE (CTRL [)	070	F	113	q
028	FS (CTRL \)	071	G	114	r
029	GS (CTRL])	072	H	115	s
030	RS (CTRL ↑)	073	I	116	t
031	US (CTRL __)	074	J	117	u
032	SPACE	075	K	118	v
033	!	076	L	119	w
034	"	077	M	120	x
035	#	078	N	121	y
036	$	079	O	122	z
037	%	080	P	123	{
038	&	081	Q	124	|
039	'	082	R	125	}
040	(	083	S	126	-
041	)	084	T	127	DEL
042	*	085	U		

LF = Line Feed; FF = Form Feed; CR = Carriage Return; DEL = Rubout; BS = Backspace; HT = Horizontal tab; VT = Vertical tab; CTRL = Control character.

FIGURE 6–1
ASCII character codes.

the ASCII code. With a convention of *even parity*, the parity bit is always set such that the total number of 1s in the 8-bit ASCII representation is *even*. With a convention of *odd parity*, the parity bit is always set such that the total number of 1s in the 8-bit ASCII representation is *odd*. Microprocessors commonly have special instructions that can test for even or odd parity. These instructions are particularly useful in testing for errors in data that, say, was transmitted over a noisy communications channel.

decimal number. The decimal number thirteen, for example, becomes:

$$0 0 0 1 0 0 1 1$$

The ability of a microprocessor to deal effectively with BCD numbers is particularly important when interfacing to a human operator. Inputs from a numeric keyboard, and outputs to numeric displays, are examples of where BCD notation is widely used. You will see (in Chap. 8) that microprocessors commonly have a special decimal adjust accumulator instruction designed specifically for dealing with BCD notation.

ASCII

ASCII (American Standard Code for Information Interchange) notation is a 7-bit code that is commonly used to represent numerals in the context of a full alphanumeric code. The four low-order bits of the code form the BCD representation of the numeral as follows:

ASCII code	Decimal number
0 1 1 0 0 0 0	0
0 1 1 0 0 0 1	1
0 1 1 0 0 1 0	2
0 1 1 0 0 1 1	3
0 1 1 0 1 0 0	4
0 1 1 0 1 0 1	5
0 1 1 0 1 1 0	6
0 1 1 0 1 1 1	7
0 1 1 1 0 0 0	8
0 1 1 1 0 0 1	9

The ASCII code representation of a number is, thus, a type of binary-coded decimal representation. Full alphanumeric keyboards, CRT displays, teletypes, and line printers are among the devices that use the ASCII code to represent numbers. A full list of the ASCII code is given in the table of Fig. 6-1.

Although only 7 bits are required to specify an ASCII character, an eighth bit is commonly added. This eighth bit is the MSB of the ASCII code and is called the *parity* bit. The parity bit can be used for *error detection* in

| Mnemonic† | | Description | Instruction code‡ | | | | | | | | Machine states § |
Z80	8080/8085		D_7	D_6	D_5	D_4	D_3	D_2	D_1	D_0	
LD r1, r2	MOV r1, r2	Move register to register	0	1	D	D	D	S	S	S	5
LD (HL), r	MOV M, r	Move register to memory	0	1	1	1	0	S	S	S	7
LD r, (HL)	MOV r, M	Move memory to register	0	1	D	D	D	1	1	0	7
HALT	HLT	Halt	0	1	1	1	0	1	1	0	7
LD r,n	MVI r, n	Move immediate register	0	0	D	D	D	1	1	0	7
LD (HL),n	MVI M, n	Move immediate memory	0	0	1	1	0	1	1	0	10
INC r	INR r	Increment register	0	0	D	D	D	1	0	0	5
DEC r	DCR r	Decrement register	0	0	D	D	D	1	0	1	5
INC (HL)	INR M	Increment memory	0	0	1	1	0	1	0	0	10
DCR (HL)	DCR M	Decrement memory	0	0	1	1	0	1	0	1	10
ADD A,r	ADD r	Add register to A	1	0	0	0	0	S	S	S	4
ADC A,r	ADC r	Add register to A with carry	1	0	0	0	1	S	S	S	4
SUB A,r	SUB r	Subtract register from A	1	0	0	1	0	S	S	S	4
SBC A,r	SBB r	Subtract register from A with borrow	1	0	0	1	1	S	S	S	4
AND r	ANA r	And register with A	1	0	1	0	0	S	S	S	4
XOR r	XRA r	Exclusive Or register with A	1	0	1	0	1	S	S	S	4

Mnemonic[†]		Description	Instruction code[‡]								Machine states[§]
Z80	8080/8085		D_7	D_6	D_5	D_4	D_3	D_2	D_1	D_0	
OR r	ORA r	Or register with A	1	0	1	1	0	S	S	S	4
CP r	CMP r	Compare register with A	1	0	1	1	1	S	S	S	4
ADD A,(HL)	ADD M	Add memory to A	1	0	0	0	0	1	1	0	7
ADC A,(HL)	ADC M	Add memory to A with carry	1	0	0	0	1	1	1	0	7
SUB A,(HL)	SUB M	Subtract memory from A	1	0	0	1	0	1	1	0	7
SBC A,(HL)	SBB M	Subtract memory from A with borrow	1	0	0	1	1	1	1	0	7
AND A,(HL)	ANA M	And memory with A	1	0	1	0	0	1	1	0	7
XOR A,(HL)	XRA M	Exclusive Or memory with A	1	0	1	0	1	1	1	0	7
OR A,(HL)	ORA M	Or memory with A	1	0	1	1	0	1	1	0	7
CP A,(HL)	CMP M	Compare memory with A	1	0	1	1	1	1	1	0	7
ADD A, n	ADI n	Add immediate to A	1	1	0	0	0	1	1	0	7
ADC A, n	ACI n	Add immediate to A with carry	1	1	0	0	1	1	1	0	7
SUB A, n	SUI n	Subtract immediate from A	1	1	0	1	0	1	1	0	7
SBC A, n	SBI n	Subtract immediate from A with borrow	1	1	0	1	1	1	1	0	7
AND A, n	ANI n	And immediate with A	1	1	1	0	0	1	1	0	7

Assembly	Machine	Description									Cycles
XOR A, n	XRI n	Exclusive Or immediate with A	1	1	1	0	1	1	1	0	7
OR A, n	ORI n	Or immediate with A	1	1	1	1	0	1	1	0	7
CP A, n	CPI n	Compare immediate with A	1	1	1	1	1	1	1	0	7
RLCA	RLC	Rotate A left	0	0	0	0	0	1	1	1	4
RRCA	RRC	Rotate A right	0	0	0	0	1	1	1	1	4
RLA	RAL	Rotate A left through carry	0	0	0	1	0	1	1	1	4
RRA	RAR	Rotate A right through carry	0	0	0	1	1	1	1	1	4
JP	JMP	Jump unconditional	1	1	0	0	0	0	1	1	10
JP C	JC	Jump on carry	1	1	0	1	1	0	1	0	10
JP NC	JNC	Jump on no carry	1	1	0	1	0	0	1	0	10
JP Z	JZ	Jump on zero	1	1	0	0	1	0	1	0	10
JP NZ	JNZ	Jump on no zero	1	1	0	0	0	0	1	0	10
JP P	JP	Jump on positive	1	1	1	1	0	0	1	0	10
JP M	JM	Jump on minus	1	1	1	1	1	0	1	0	10
JP PE	JPE	Jump on parity even	1	1	1	0	1	0	1	0	10
JP PO	JPO	Jump on parity odd	1	1	1	0	0	0	1	0	10
CALL	CALL	Call unconditional	1	1	0	0	1	1	0	1	17

Mnemonic		Description	Instruction code‡								Machine states §
Z80	8080/8085		D_7	D_6	D_5	D_4	D_3	D_2	D_1	D_0	
CALL C	CC	Call on carry	1	1	0	1	1	1	0	0	11/17
CALL NC	CNC	Call on no carry	1	1	0	1	0	1	0	0	11/17
CALL Z	CZ	Call on zero	1	1	0	0	1	1	0	0	11/17
CALL NZ	CNZ	Call on no zero	1	1	0	0	0	1	0	0	11/17
CALL P	CP	Call on positive	1	1	1	1	0	1	0	0	11/17
CALL M	CM	Call on minus	1	1	1	1	1	1	0	0	11/17
CALL PE	CPE	Call on parity even	1	1	1	0	1	1	0	0	11/17
CALL PO	CPO	Call on parity odd	1	1	1	0	0	1	0	0	11/17
RET	RET	Return	1	1	0	0	1	0	0	1	10
RET C	RC	Return on carry	1	1	0	1	1	0	0	0	5/11
RET NC	RNC	Return on no carry	1	1	0	1	0	0	0	0	5/11
RET Z	RZ	Return on zero	1	1	0	0	1	0	0	0	5/11
RET NC	RNZ	Return on no zero	1	1	0	0	0	0	0	0	5/11
RET P	RP	Return on positive	1	1	1	1	0	0	0	0	5/11
RET M	RM	Return on minus	1	1	1	1	1	0	0	0	5/11
RET PE	RPE	Return on parity even	1	1	1	0	1	0	0	0	5/11
RET PO	RPO	Return on parity odd	1	1	1	0	0	0	0	0	5/11
RST	RST	Restart	1	1	X	Y	Z	1	1	1	11
IN A,(n)	IN n	Input from port n	1	1	0	1	1	0	1	1	10*

											10*
OUT (n),A	OUT n	Output to port n	1	1	0	1	0	0	1	1	10*
LD BC,nn	LXI B, nn	Load immediate register Pair B & C	0	0	0	0	0	0	0	1	10
LD DE,nn	LXI D, nn	Load immediate register Pair D & E	0	0	0	1	0	0	0	1	10
LD HL,nn	LXI H, nn	Load immediate register Pair H & L	0	0	1	0	0	0	0	1	10
LD SP,nn	LXI SP, nn	Load immediate stack pointer	0	0	1	1	0	0	0	1	10
PUSH BC	PUSH B	Push register Pair B & C on stack	1	1	0	0	0	1	0	1	11
PUSH DE	PUSH D	Push register Pair D & E on stack	1	1	0	1	0	1	0	1	11
PUSH HL	PUSH H	Push register Pair H & L on stack	1	1	1	0	0	1	0	1	11
PUSH AF	PUSH PSW	Push A and Flags on stack	1	1	1	1	0	1	0	1	11
POP BC	POP B	Pop register pair B & C off stack	1	1	0	0	0	0	0	1	10
POP DE	POP D	Pop register pair D & E off stack	1	1	0	1	0	0	0	1	10
POP HL	POP H	Pop register pair H & L off stack	1	1	1	0	0	0	0	1	10
POP AF	POP PSW	Pop A and Flags off stack	1	1	1	1	0	0	0	1	10
LD (nn), A	STA nn	Store A direct	0	0	1	1	0	0	1	0	13

Mnemonic† Z80	8080/8085	Description	D_7	D_6	D_5	D_4	D_3	D_2	D_1	D_0	Machine states §
LD A, (nn)	LDA nn	Load A direct	0	0	1	1	1	0	1	0	13
EX DE,HL	XCHG	Exchange D & E, H & L Registers	1	1	1	0	1	0	1	1	4
EX (SP),HL	XTHL	Exchange top of stack, H & L	1	1	1	0	0	0	1	1	18
LD SP,HL	SPHL	H & L to stack pointer	1	1	1	1	1	0	0	1	5
JP (HL)	PCHL	H & L to program counter	1	1	1	0	1	0	0	1	5
ADD HL,BC	DAD B	Add B & C to H & L	0	0	0	0	1	0	0	1	10
ADD HL,DE	DAD D	Add D & E to H & L	0	0	0	1	1	0	0	1	10
ADD HL,HL	DAD H	Add H & L to H & L	0	0	1	0	1	0	0	1	10
ADD HL,SP	DAD SP	Add stack pointer to H & L	0	0	1	1	1	0	0	1	10
LD (BC),A	STAX B	Store A indirect	0	0	0	0	0	0	1	0	7
LD (DE),A	STAX D	Store A indirect	0	0	0	1	0	0	1	0	7
LD A,(BC)	LDAX B	Load A indirect	0	0	0	0	1	0	1	0	7
LD A,(DE)	LDAX D	Load A indirect	0	0	0	1	1	0	1	0	7
INC BC	INX B	Increment B & C registers	0	0	0	0	0	0	1	1	5
INC DE	INX D	Increment D & E registers	0	0	0	1	0	0	1	1	5
INC HL	INX H	Increment H & L registers	0	0	1	0	0	0	1	1	5
INC SP	INX SP	Increment stack pointer	0	0	1	1	0	0	1	1	5
DEC BC	DCX B	Decrement B & C	0	0	0	0	1	0	1	1	5

DEC DE	DCX D	Decrement D & E	0	0	0	1	1	0	1	5
DEC HL	DCX H	Decrement H & L	0	0	1	0	1	0	1	5
DEC SP	DCX SP	Decrement stack pointer	0	0	1	1	0	1	1	5
CPL	CMA	Complement A	0	0	1	0	1	1	1	4
SCF	STC	Set carry	0	0	1	1	0	1	1	4
CCF	CMC	Complement carry	0	0	1	1	1	1	1	4
DAA	DAA	Decimal adjust A	0	0	1	0	0	1	1	4
LD (nn),HL	SHLD nn	Store H & L direct	0	0	1	0	0	1	0	16
LD HL,(nn)	LHLD nn	Load H & L direct	0	0	1	0	1	1	0	16
EI	EI	Enable Interrupts	1	1	1	1	0	1	1	4
DI	DI	Disable interrupts	1	1	1	0	0	1	1	4
NOP	NOP	No-operation	0	0	0	0	0	0	0	4

†M and (HL) refer to the memory location at address given by the contents of the H, L register. PSW is the "program status word," which is the 16-bit word made up of the flag register and accumulator.

‡DDD or SSS: 000 B; 001 C; 010 D; 011 E; 100 H; 101 L; 110 Memory; 111 A.

§ Two possible cycle times (5/11) indicate instruction cycles dependent on condition flags.

*Input and output require 10 states for the 8080 or 8085 but requires 11 states for the Z80 microprocessor.

FIGURE 6-2

Machine language instructions common to the 8080, 8085, and Z80 microprocessors.

MACHINE LANGUAGE PROGRAMMING

While the machine language instruction set varies from one microprocessor to another, the instructions listed in Fig. 6-2 are common to several microprocessors, including the 8080, 8085, and Z80. This listing is, in fact, the 8080 instruction set and a subset of the instructions available to the 8085 and Z80. Manufacturers of the 8080 and 8085 use a different set of mnemonics for these instructions than do the manufacturers of the Z80. Both sets of mnemonics are listed in Fig. 6-2.

To illustrate how machine language instructions can be used to construct a microprocessor program, consider a simple program to accept 8 bits of data from an input port, and subsequently output these 8 bits of data to an output port. The first instruction of the program required to do this is an *input instruction* which (from Fig. 6-2) is coded in machine language as:

$$1\ 1\ 0\ 1\ 1\ 0\ 1\ 1$$

This instruction must be followed by a second byte of information to specify one of 256 possible input ports. To input from port 1, for example, would require the following code:

$$1\ 1\ 0\ 1\ 1\ 0\ 1\ 1$$
$$0\ 0\ 0\ 0\ 0\ 0\ 0\ 1$$

The second instruction of this example program is an output instruction. To output to port 3 would take the following code:

$$1\ 1\ 0\ 1\ 0\ 0\ 1\ 1$$
$$0\ 0\ 0\ 0\ 0\ 0\ 1\ 1$$

Using hex notation, for compactness, the entire program can now be written as:

$$\text{DB}$$
$$\text{01}$$
$$\text{D3}$$
$$\text{03}$$

Each byte of the 4-byte program requires one memory location. If the program starts at location 0000H in memory, each byte would have the following memory locations:

Memory location	Memory contents
0000H	DB
0001H	01
0002H	D3
0003H	03

Now suppose the output port is to be continually updated with the current data at the input port. To do this, a *program loop* is created by adding a *jump instruction* to the program. The program now becomes:

Memory location	Contents	Description
0001H	DB	Input
0002H	01	from port 1
0003H	D3	Output
0004H	03	to port 3
0005H	C3	Jump to
0006H	00	location 00 (eight low-order bits)
0007H	00	00 (eight high-order bits)

The operation of this program is shown diagrammatically in Fig. 6-3. Following the application of a reset pulse to the microprocessor, program execution begins automatically at memory location 0000H. The first instruction calls for data to be input from port 1. This data is stored internally in the microprocessor in an 8-bit register called the *accumulator*. Next, the microprocessor reads the second instruction in memory, and executes this instruction by outputting the information in the accumulator to output port 3. The third instruction of the program causes the program to begin again at location 0000H, and the cycle repeats.

It is easy to calculate the time required for the execution of a single loop of the example program. Notice that in Fig. 6-2 the number of clock cycles (machine states) required for each instruction is shown. For an 8080 with a 2-MHz clock, each clock cycle requires 0.5 μs. Each of the three instruc-

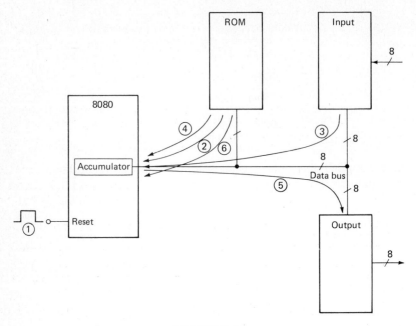

FIGURE 6-3

Sequential execution of the sample program. 1 A logic pulse is used to reset the microprocessor to begin program execution at location 0000H in memory. 2 The first and second bytes of memory are read. These two bytes tell the microprocessor to input from input port number 01. 3 Data is input from port number 01. It is stored in the accumulator inside the microprocessor. 4 The next two bytes are read from memory. These tell the microprocessor to output the contents of the accumulator to output port 03. 5 Data is output to the output port. 6 The next three bytes of memory are read. These three bytes constitute the jump to zero instruction. The processor resets its program counter to zero, and the sequence begins again at step 2.

tions in the example program requires 10 clock cycles. The total time required for a single loop through the program is

$$(10 + 10 + 10) \times 0.5 \ \mu s = 15 \ \mu s$$

Exactly half the time would be required if a 4-MHz clock were used in place of the 2-MHz clock.

MACHINE CYCLES

Every microprocessor program is executed as a series of *machine cycles*. Each machine cycle can be further divided into a number of *machine states.* For the 8080 microprocessor, each instruction may consist of one, two, three, four, or five machine cycles. These cycles are designated as M1, M2, M3, M4, and M5. Each machine cycle may consist of three, four, or five states. The states within the machine cycle are designated as T1, T2, T3, T4, and T5. The duration of each state is equal to the period of the microprocessor clock.

Returning to the example program, consider the detailed events that occur during execution of each instruction. The first instruction is an *input instruction* that occurs in 3 machine cycles and 10 states as shown below:

	T1	T2	T3	T4
M1	Address 0000H put on address bus	READY line interrogated	Data transfer: DB on data bus	Instruction decoding
M2	Address 0001H put on address bus	READY line interrogated	Data transfer: 01 on data bus	
M3	Address 0101H put on data bus	READY line interrogated	Data transfer: input data on data bus	

Since 10 states are used, the execution time for this instruction is 5 μs, assuming a 2-MHz clock.

Notice that during T1 of each machine cycle address information is put on the address bus. During M1, this is the address of the first byte (or *op code*) of the instruction. During M2, this is the address of the second byte of the instruction. During M3, this is the address of the input port (which is duplicated in both the eight high-order and eight low-order bits of the address by the 8080).

During T2 of each machine cycle, the READY line is interrogated. If it is high, the microprocessor proceeds to T3. If it is low, the micro-processor inserts *wait states* between T2 and T3 until the READY line does go high.

During T3, data transfer occurs. For the case of the 2-byte input instruction, it is the instruction itself that is transferred from memory to the microprocessor during T3 of M1 and M2. During M3, the input data is transferred from the input port to the microprocessor accumulator.

Only an M1 cycle may have a T4 or a T5 state. During this time, the microprocessor decodes the op code (first byte of the instruction) to establish the nature of the subsequent machine cycles.

The second instruction in example program is an *output instruction*. The detailed execution of this instruction is shown below:

	T1	T2	T3	T4
M1	Address = 0002H	READY line interrogated	Data transfer: data = D3	Instruction decoding
M2	Address = 0003H	READY line interrogated	Data transfer: data = 03	
M3	Address = 0303H	READY line interrogated	Data transfer: output data	

The operation of the output instruction is very much analogous to the operation of the input instruction. During T3 of M3, however, data is *output* from the accumulator to the output port. Execution of the input instruction and output instruction by the Z80 microprocessor differs from that of the 8080 in that a wait state is automatically inserted between the T2 and T3 state of the M3 machine cycle. This is to allow more time for data transfer to and from I10 ports. Execution of these instructions by the Z80 requires 11 states rather than 10.

The third instruction in the sample program is a *jump instruction* that is executed as follows:

	T1	T2	T3	T4
M1	Address = 0004	READY line interrogated	Data transfer: data = C3	Instruction decoding
M2	Address = 0005	READY line interrogated	Data transfer: data = 00	
M3	Address = 0006	READY line interrogated	Data transfer: data = 00	

REGISTERS

The RAM within the microprocessor itself is commonly organized in *registers*. One such register is the accumulator. A diagram of the registers available in the Z80 microprocessor is shown in Fig. 3-9. Most of the machine language instructions for microprocessors are designed to move data to and from registers or to manipulate data that is stored in registers.

Referring to Fig. 6-2, what is the machine language code (in hex) for the instruction that moves the contents of the accumulator (source register) to the B register (destination register)?

Answer　47H

Within a microprocessor there is very often a *flag register* composed of a set of *flag bits*. These bits are set and reset during the course of a microprocessor program to record specific conditions in instruction execution. The information stored by the flag bits represents useful information that can be called on by the microprocessor program.

The flag bits of the 8080 microprocessor are representative of those found in other microprocessors. These flag bits are:

1. zero

2. sign

3. parity

4. carry

5. auxiliary carry

The zero flag is set to a logic 1 if the result of an instruction is zero; otherwise the zero flag is reset to a logic 0. The sign flag is set if the MSB of the result of an instruction is one; otherwise it is reset. The parity flag is set if the result of an instruction is a number with even parity; otherwise it is reset. The carry flag is set if an instruction resulted in a carry (from addition) or a borrow (from subtraction); otherwise it is reset. The auxiliary carry flag is set if an instruction results in a carry from bit 3 to bit 4. This flag is used in BCD arithmetic as described in Chap. 8.

ADDRESSING MODES

One measure of the effectiveness of a microprocessor's instruction set is the number of available *addressing modes*. There are a number of different ways a memory location may be specified in a microprocessor instruction, and each way is a different addressing mode.

The most obvious way to specify an address in an instruction is to include the entire 16-bit address as two bytes of the instruction. This is called *direct addressing*. Another method of addressing occurs when a 16-bit pointer register (such as the HL register) holds the address of the desired memory location. This is called *register-indirect addressing*. A memory location may also be specified in an instruction relative to an *index register*, where the displacement from the index register address is given in the instruction. This is called *indexed addressing*. An instruction may also specify a memory location relative to its own location in memory. This is called *relative addressing*. Data that is stored in an internal microprocessor register may be addressed. This is called *register addressing*. Finally, an instruction may refer to data that immediately follows the op code of the instruction. This is called *immediate addressing*.

All of the above addressing modes are used by various instructions of the Z80 and 8748 microprocessors. All but indexed and relative addressing are used by the 8080 microprocessor.

STACK OPERATIONS

In general, information may be stored in and retrieved from RAM in an arbitrary order. However, one particularly useful method of organizing information in memory is as a last-in first-out (LIFO) or *stack* structure. Consider, for example, a stack of pancakes. The first pancake placed on the stack is the last one you eat, while the last pancake placed on the stack is the first one you eat. Similarly, in a microprocessor system, the last information to be stored in a stack memory is the first to be retrieved. When information is stored on the stack it is said to be *pushed* onto the stack. When information is retrieved from the stack it is said to be *popped* from it.

Some microprocessors have an internal memory used specifically for stacking information. Other microprocessors use a portion of external memory space for this function. When external memory is used, an internal register of the microprocessor called the *stack pointer* holds the address of the top of the stack. The stack is commonly stored upside down in memory. As data is pushed onto the stack, it is stored at progressively lower memory addresses. As a result, the *top* of the stack is its *lowest* memory address.

The stack memory is most commonly used for storing information about the state of the microprocessor just prior to branching to a subroutine or an interrupt service routine. The information can be retrieved from the stack upon completion of the subroutine to restore the microprocessor to the state it was in just prior to branching to the subroutine. One important piece of information, for example, is the value of the program counter prior to branching to a subroutine (since this is the *return address* to which the microprocessor must return upon completion of the subroutine).

When writing programs for microprocessors such as the 8080 or Z80 that use external memory space for the stack, it is crucial that the value of the stack pointer be set by the microprocessor program prior to any stack operations. In fact, it is a good programming practice to have the load stack pointer instruction as the very first instruction of the microprocessor program. The value of the stack pointer register is then automatically decremented prior to every stack write operation and incremented following every stack read operation.

Example

Given a Z80 microprocessor system with a total of 4K of RAM beginning at location 0000H in memory space, what address should be loaded into the stack pointer to assure that the stack is stored at the very top of available memory space?

Answer 1000H. *Note:* Since the stack pointer is decremented *prior* to each stack write operation, the first element in the stack is stored at location 0FFFH, which is the highest memory address in the first 4K of memory.

SUBROUTINES

A subroutine is a portion of a microprocessor program that may be branched to or "called" from other parts of the program. Subroutines are called by a call instruction followed by the starting address of the subroutine. Subroutines are terminated by a return instruction. When a subroutine is called, the address of the next instruction following the call instruction is pushed onto the stack as the *return address*. The return instruction causes the return address to be popped off of the stack and loaded into the program counter so that the main program can resume. Note that the LIFO structure of the stack permits subroutine *nesting*; subroutines can be called from within subroutines which can call further subroutines and so on.

To illustrate the operation of the call instruction it is useful to expand the call instruction in cycle-by-cycle detail as with simpler instructions earlier in this chapter. For the purposes of illustration, assume that the stack is stored at the top of a 4K memory space and that the address of the subroutine being called is 0200H. The following program is used to load the stack pointer and call the subroutine (all numbers are in hexadecimal):

Memory address	Contents	Comment
0000	31	Load SP
0001	00	Low byte
0002	10	High byte
0003	CD	Call
0004	00	Low byte
0005	02	High byte

Notice that the return address is 0006 since this is the address of the next instruction following the call. Referring to Fig. 6-4 you see that the call instruction requires five machine cycles for a total of 17 states. M1 is used to fetch the instruction op code. M2 and M3 are used to read the second and third bytes of the instruction which give the address of the beginning of the subroutine being called. M4 and M5 are used for stack write operations to store the return address on the stack.

FIGURE 6–4

The execution of the call instruction requires five machine cycles and seventeen machine states. M1 is the instruction op code fetch. M2 and M3 are used to read the second and third bytes of the instruction (the subroutine address). M4 and M5 are used to push the return address onto the stack. Upon completion of the call instruction, the next operation is an M1 cycle at the beginning of the subroutine.

	T1	T2	T3	T4	T5
M1	Addr = 0003	Ready?	Data = CD	Instruction decoding	
M2	Addr = 0004	Ready?	Data = 00		
M3	Addr = 0005	Ready?	Data = 02		
M4	Addr = OFFF	Ready?	Data = 00		
M5	Addr = OFFE	Ready?	Data = 06		
M1	Addr = 0200	. . .			

The restart instruction is similar to the call instruction but it is only one byte long. The restart instruction has the general form of 11*XYZ*11 and is able to specify one of eight subroutine locations depending on the values of *X, Y,* and *Z.* The instruction is equivalent to the following 3-byte call instruction:

$$1\ 1\ 0\ 0\ 1\ 1\ 0\ 1$$
$$0\ 0\ X\ Y\ Z\ 0\ 0\ 0$$
$$0\ 0\ 0\ 0\ 0\ 0\ 0\ 0$$

As described in Chap. 5, the restart instruction is commonly used following an interrupt to branch to an interrupt service routine.

EXERCISES

6-1 Give the twos complement, in hexadecimal notation, of each of these hex numbers:

a. 7F   b. 00   c. 66   d. 11   e. 0F

6-2 Write the following decimal numbers in 8-bit BCD notation:

a. 56   b. 70   c. 99   d. 4   e. 32

6-3 What symbols are represented by the following ASCII code (given in hex):

a. 33   b. 40   c. 61   d. 4F   e. 5C

6-4 In the ASCII code given in Exercise 6-3, it is assumed that the parity bit is equal to zero. What would the ASCII code for each character be if the parity bit were set to assure even parity in each case? Give answers in hexadecimal notation.

6-5 What is the machine language code (in hex) for the instruction of Fig. 6-2 used to transfer the contents of the C register to the B register?

6-6 What is the machine language code (in hex) for the instruction of Fig. 6-2 used to transfer the contents of the D register to the accumulator?

6-7 Referring to the manufacturer's literature for a specific microprocessor, give examples of machine language instructions that make use of the following addressing modes: (a) direct, (b) register-indirect, (c) indexed, (d) relative, (e) register, (f) immediate.

6-8   What are the addresses of the stack locations used and the contents of those locations following the execution of the following machine language code: 31 FF FF CD 03 00? Assume that the program starts at location 0600H in memory space. Assuming a processor with a 4-MHz clock, what is the total execution time of the machine code?

6-9   Given a microprocessor system with 30 K of RAM (beginning at location 0000H), what should the second and third byte of the load stack pointer instruction be to assure the stack resides at the very top of memory space?

6-10 A Z80 microprocessor using mode 0 interrupts (8080 mode) has the following hardware (see figure below) as the interrupt service port. What is the starting address in memory of the interrupt service routine?

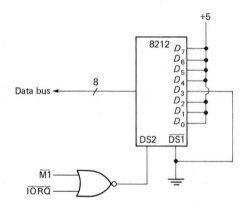

7

ASSEMBLY AND HIGH-LEVEL LANGUAGES

For all but the simplest programs, writing in machine language is a chore. As a result, higher level languages have been developed to facilitate the development of microprocessor programs. Programming languages can be divided, somewhat arbitrarily, into four hierarchical levels:

	Microprogram language	Machine-oriented
	Machine language	
	Assembly language	
People-oriented	High-level language	

The *microprogram language* is normally invisible to the user of a microprocessor: the microprogram is resident inside the microprocessor. The microprogram interprets the machine language instructions received by the microprocessor, and is responsible for the proper execution of these instructions. Some microprocessors are *user microprogrammable*. This means that the user of the microprocessor can specify the microprogram, and, thus, design a custom *instruction set*. Most microprocessors are not user microprogrammable, and thus have a *fixed instruction set*.

Machine language, as described previously, consists of a set of instructions that the microprocessor is able to execute. The nature of the instruction set is determined by the internal *architecture* of the microprocessor and its internal microprogram.

Assembly language and *high-level languages* consist of a set of statements that are more easily understood by people than are machine language instructions. As shown in Fig. 7-1, these statements must first be translated into machine language before they can be properly executed by

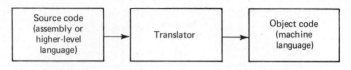

FIGURE 7-1
A translator is used to convert the source code to the object
code.

FIGURE 7-2
Development system. (*Cromemco Incorporated.*)

a microprocessor. This translation is done by a *translator*. A translator that converts assembly language into machine language is called an *assembler*. Translators that convert high-level languages, such as Fortran or Basic, into machine language are called *compilers* or *interpreters*.

Assembly or high-level language that is input to a translator is called *source code*. The machine language output of a translator is called *object code*. The translator itself is a computer program that creates object code from source code. If the translator program executes on a computer for which it produces object code, it is said to be a *resident translator*. If the translator program executes on a machine other than the one for which it produces object code, it is said to be a *cross translator*.

A microprocessor system that is used primarily for program development, namely editing source code and translating this source code to machine language object code, is called a *development system*. A development system normally includes a disk drive for program storage, a CRT terminal for entering and displaying data, a printer for hard-copy output, a PROM programmer for burning object code into UV erasable PROMs, and resident editing and translating programs. One such development system is shown in Fig. 7-2.

ASSEMBLY LANGUAGE

The instruction set used in writing an assembly language program is identical to the instruction set used in writing programs in machine language. For this reason, assembly language is not considered a high-level language, although it does have several important features that make program development in assembly language much easier than program development directly in machine code. Three of these features are (1) *mnemonics* are used rather than numbers to specify instructions, (2) *labels* may be used in place of absolute memory addresses or other numbers, and (3) *pseudo ops* may be used to provide special instructions to the assembler.

Every statement in an assembly language program is made up of four parts or *fields*. These are the (1) label field, (2) instruction mnemonic field, (3) operand field, and (4) comment field. Taking the example program of Chap. 6 that inputs data from port 1 and outputs this data to port 3, you could write the program in assembly language using Z80 mnemonics in this way:

Label	Mnemonic	Operand(s)	Comments
NAME:	IN	A,01	;INPUT FROM PORT 1
	OUT	03,A	;OUTPUT TO PORT 3
	JP	NAME	;KEEP GOING

A semicolon is used to separate the operand field from the comment field. The comment field itself is ignored by the assembler but is used by the programmer and others as an aid to understanding the program.

Now, in looking at this example assembly language program, it is clear that the assembler has not been given adequate information to assemble the source code. The assembler must know where the program is to reside in memory space. Only in this way will the assembler be able to assign a proper absolute address to the label NAME. The *origin address* of the program in memory is specified by a special ORG statement in the assembly language program. The ORG statement is called a pseudo operation or *pseudo op* since the statement is not translated into machine language code, but rather provides the assembler with specific information required in the process of translating the assembly language program.

Depending on the design of the specific assembler being used, other pseudo ops may be available to the programmer. Another common pseudo op is the equate or EQU pseudo op. Using this pseudo op, the programmer can equate a label to a specific numeric value. In the case of the example program, suppose that the information at input port 1 was digitally-encoded heart rate information, and suppose that output port 3 was connected to an instrument panel display. Using pseudo ops, the assembly language program could be written in this way:

```
          ORG    0000H
RATE:     EQU    01
DISPLAY:  EQU    03
NAME:     IN     A,RATE
          OUT    DISPLAY,A
          JP     NAME
```

The ORG statement is used to specify that the program is to begin at location 0000H in memory space. The EQU statements equate the labels RATE and DISPLAY to the numbers 1 and 3 respectively. The program inputs rate information into the accumulator, outputs the accumulator to the display, and loops. Comments are optional and not included here.

While the value of using labels may not be apparent in a very short program, in a long program, consisting of thousands of lines of code, the use of mnemonic labels can spell the difference between readable code and a numeric nightmare. Good programming practice dictates the liberal use of labels and comments in assembly language programming.

Many assemblers have a number of other features that aid assembly language program development. These features include *macros, conditional assembly*, and *relocatable object code.*

If one group of statements is used many times in a single program, a *macro* may be defined to specify that group of statements. A macro saves a programmer from listing the entire set of statements each time they are required in the program. The use of macros improves program readability and eliminates the need for rewriting repetitive blocks of code in a program.

As an example of a macro definition, suppose that in the course of a program you have need to exchange the upper and lower four bits of the accumulator. This can be done by using the rotate left circular accumulator instruction four times in succession. If this operation were to be used many times during the course of a program, you could define the operation as a macro in the following way:

```
ROTATE:   MACRO
          RLCA
          RLCA
          RLCA
          RLCA
          MEND
```

In this example, ROTATE is the *name* of the macro. The four RLCA instructions compose the *body* of the macro. The MEND pseudo op is a *delimiter* used to terminate the macro definition. Once a macro has been defined, the macro name may be used just like any other instruction in the assembly language program. The assembler will automatically *expand* the macro by replacing the macro name by the body of the macro given in the macro definition.

Many assemblers allow parameters to be transferred by a macro. Referring to the previous example, you could define a macro that would input data from port 1 and output the data to port 3 in the following way:

```
INOUT:    MACRO
          IN        A,01
          OUT       03,A
          MEND
```

But, suppose you wanted to be able to input and output data from any of the 256 possible ports, and not be limited to ports 1 and 3. This is done by using parameters to represent the port addresses and transferring the value of these parameters as operands of the macro name. Using the labels #INPORT for the input port address and #OUTPORT for the output port address, the macro is defined in the following way:

```
INOUT:    MACRO     #INPORT,#OUTPORT
          IN        A,#INPORT
          OUT       #OUTPORT,A
          MEND
```

The prefix "#" is used to distinguish macro parameter labels from other labels in the program. Now, any two ports may be specified as operands of the INOUT macro. If, for example, you did want to specify ports 1 and 3, you would write:

```
          INOUT     1,3
```

Macros allow you to use an assembler designed for one microprocessor as an assembler for other microprocessors. A Z80 macro assembler, for example, can be used to assemble 6800 source code simply by defining the mnemonics for the 6800 instruction set as macros in the Z80 assembler. The operands of the 6800 instructions are transferred as parameters to the body of the macro.

It is important to note how a macro differs from a subroutine. The macro is expanded by the assembler. The machine language code of the macro body appears everywhere in the program the macro is used. The machine language code of a subroutine, by contrast, appears only once in the program. A subroutine call causes the program to branch to this machine language code. The advantage of using macros is that they can be executed more quickly than subroutines since no program branching is required. The advantage of subroutines is that less memory space is required for the program since the subroutine code appears only once.

Conditional assembly, a feature offered by some assemblers, enables an assembler to selectively assemble or not assemble certain blocks of code depending on whether certain conditions are true or false. An IF pseudo op is used to check if the condition is true or false. The block of code that is conditionally assembled is bounded by the IF pseudo op and the ENDIF pseudo op. To illustrate how conditional assembly can be used, suppose you wish to define a macro that rotates the contents of the accumulator three positions to the right or left depending on whether the operand of the macro is an R or an L. Naming the macro ROTAT3, here is how it can be done:

```
ROTAT3:     MACRO     #DIREC
            IF        '#DIREC' EQ 'R'
            RRCA
            RRCA
            RRCA
            ENDIF
            IF        '#DIREC' EQ 'L'
            RLCA
            RLCA
            RLCA
            ENDIF
            MEND
```

The operand of an IF statement may be an expression, as in the above example, or a label. The operand is considered false if it is zero and true otherwise. The statements between the IF and ENDIF statements are assembled only when the operand of the IF statement is true.

Another feature available in some assemblers is the ability to produce *relocatable object code* rather than *absolute object code*. Absolute object code is able to begin executing at only one specific memory location, namely the location specified by the ORG statement in the assembly language source code. Relocatable object code, however, contains additional information on all address-dependent references in the object code. A special *relocating loader* program is able to interpret this additional information and load the relocatable object code beginning at any desired memory address. Relocatable code is particularly useful when linking subroutines from a subroutine library to a main program. The subroutines can be conveniently abutted to the end of the main program without having to reassemble the subroutine source code.

PL/M

While assembly language does greatly simplify the composition of micro-processor programs, high-level languages make the job even easier. PL/M was the first high-level language developed specifically for microproces-sor systems. The translator used to convert PL/M source code into machine language is called a PL/M *compiler*. Writing programs in a high-level language such as PL/M can greatly reduce program development time, but may not produce the most efficient object code. A skilled programmer writing in assembly language usually can generate more compact and faster executing code than can be generated by a compiler from a high-level language.

To illustrate the use of the PL/M language, consider a couple of simple programs written in PL/M. For the first example, consider a program designed to input a byte of data from input port 0FH, divide the number by two, and output the quotient to output port 0FH. A binary number can be divided by two simply by shifting the number one place to the right. You could write a program in assembly language to do this using Z80 mnemonics as follows:

```
IN    A 0FH    ;INPUT FROM PORT 0F
SCF            ;SET CARRY FLAG = 1
CCF            ;COMPLEMENT CARRY FLAG
RRA            :ROTATE RIGHT ACCUMULATOR
OUT   0FH,A    :OUTPUT TO PORT 0F
```

The carry flag is set to 1 and then complemented to assure that a 0 is rotated into the MSB of the accumulator by the rotate right accumulator instruction. When assembled, this program would produce the following object code:

$$\text{DB} \quad \text{0F} \quad 37 \quad \text{3F} \quad \text{1F} \quad \text{D3} \quad \text{0F}$$

If you were to write this program in PL/M, it would take just one line of code to do what took five lines of assembly language:

$$\text{OUTPUT(0FH)} = \text{SHR(INPUT(0FH),1)}$$

This line of code reads: shift right the number at input port 0F by one position and output the result to port 0F. If you were to pass this line of code through a PL/M compiler it would generate the following object code:

$$\text{DB} \quad \text{0F} \quad \text{B7} \quad \text{1F} \quad \text{D3} \quad \text{0F}$$

Something interesting has happened here. The compiler has actually produced more compact code than the assembly language program. The compiler used just one instruction (B7, OR the accumulator with itself) to reset the carry bit rather than the two instructions used in the assembly language program (SCF and CCF).

Before giving the PL/M compiler too much credit though, suppose you had written the PL/M program in a different but perfectly acceptable way:

OUTPUT(0FH) = (INPUT(0FH))/2

This statement, when compiled, results in nearly one hundred bytes of object code. The particular PL/M compiler used to compile this statement invoked a complicated division algorithm at the sight of the division symbol even though all that was required was a simple rotate operation.

To develop an appreciation for the power of the PL/M language, consider the PL/M solution to a problem of binary to BCD conversion: converting a 16-bit number to four BCD digits and outputing these four digits to output ports 4 and 5. The PL/M program looks like this:

```
            DECLARE FLAG BYTE, (NUMBER, FACTOR, BCDR)
                                    ADDRESS
    FLAG = 1;
    FACTOR = 1;
    BCDR = NUMBER MOD 10;
    DO WHILE FLAG < > 4;
        NUMBER = (NUMBER−NUMBER MOD 10)/10;
        FACTOR = FACTOR * 16;
        BCDR = BCDR + FACTOR * (NUMBER MOD 10);
        FLAG = FLAG + 1;
        END;
    OUTPUT(4) = LOW(BCDR);
    OUTPUT(5) = HIGH(BCDR);
```

The first statement of this program informs the compiler that four variables are used in the program. FLAG is an 8-bit (or byte) variable. NUMBER, FACTOR, and BCDR are 16-bit (or ADDRESS) variables. FLAG and FACTOR are initialized to have the value 1. BCDR is initialized to be the remainder when NUMBER is divided by 10 (i.e., NUMBER modulo 10). Then, a loop is iterated as long as FLAG is not equal to 4. FLAG is incremented at the end of each loop (FLAG = FLAG + 1). Each iteration produces one BCD digit. Finally, these BCD digits are output to ports 4 and 5. When this PL/M program is compiled, the resultant machine language program takes approximately 300 bytes.

This BCD conversion routine is very useful when, for example, you want to use a microprocessor to drive a numeric display. Each BCD number can be used to drive one display device, as shown in Fig. 7-3.

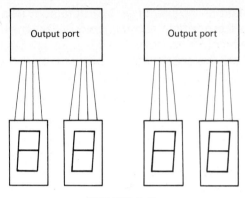

FIGURE 7–3
BCD output can be used to drive LED
displays.

BASIC

Basic is a high-level language that has become very popular for use with microprocessors. The translator program normally used with Basic is an *interpreter* rather than a compiler. The distinction between a compiler and an interpreter is that the interpreter translates the high-level language *at the time of execution* into the appropriate machine language instructions. Both the source code and the interpreter must be present in the microprocessor system at the time of execution. A compiler, by contrast, generates machine language code off-line. It is this object code that is executed, and neither the compiler itself nor the source code need be called upon at the time of execution.

Interpreters are generally less sophisticated than compilers. In an interpretive system, more memory space is required at the time of execution, and the execution time is generally longer than is the case for machine code generated by an optimized compiler. Interpreters do allow an operator more direct interaction with the computer however, since source code can be executed immediately on a line-by-line basis as it is entered into the computer.

Basic interpreters vary greatly in capability. At one extreme are the interpreters requiring just 2K or 3K of microprocessor memory and limited to integer arithmetic. These interpreters can be very useful in control applications and in low-cost microprocessor systems where a high-level language is needed. At the other extreme are extended Basic interpreters with full 14-digit, floating-point arithmetic capability, transcendental functions, and matrix operations. Extended Basic interpreters generally require 16K or more of memory space.

As an illustration of the use of a Basic program in a microprocessor system, return to the example of a binary to BCD conversion routine. The following Basic program is designed to input an 8-bit binary number between 0 and 99 (decimal) from input port 1, and output the BCD equivalent at output port 1. The program is written in a 3K integer Basic.*

$$OUT(1) = (IN(1)/10) * 16 + IN(1) - (IN(1)/10) * 10$$

Just one statement is required to perform the conversion. Since this is an integer-only Basic, the value at input port 1 is divided by 10 to find the most significant digit, then multiplied by 16 to shift this digit to the high-order 4 bits of the byte. The low-order digit is found by subtracting 10 times the high-order digit from the number at the input port.

For one more example, here is a Basic program that calculates the prime numbers between 1 and 10,000. The PRINT statements in this program output the calculated prime numbers to a console or printer that is interfaced to the microprocessor system.

```
10 PRINT 1
20 PRINT 2
30 FOR N = 3 TO 10000
40 FOR I = 2 TO N/2
50 IF N = (N/I) * I GOTO 80
60 NEXT I
70 PRINT N
80 NEXT N
```

The first two prime numbers are explicitly printed out by the first two statements of the program. Subsequent numbers N are tested for being prime by testing to see if they are exactly divisible by any integer I. If any N is exactly divisible by any I, it is discarded.

OTHER HIGH-LEVEL LANGUAGES

In addition to PL/M and Basic, a number of other high-level languages are used with microprocessor systems, each having unique advantages.

Fortran, which is an acronym for "formula translator," was one of the first high-level compiler languages developed for large mainframe computers (by IBM Corporation). As such, many application programs are available written in this language. The Fortran source code has also been standardized by the American National Standards Institute (ANSI) assuring that ANSI standard code written for one computer system will execute properly

*Cromemco 3K Control Basic.

on other systems. No such complete standard exists for Basic. Fortran compilers available for microprocessor systems are used primarily for calculations in scientific and engineering applications.

Cobol is a compiler language used mainly in business and data processing applications. Like Fortran, Cobol benefits from an ANSI standard definition. Because of its wide-spread use in business systems, Cobol is one of the most common languages used for programming large computers, and has only recently been adapted for use on microprocessor systems. In business applications, Cobol is rivaled only by RPG-2 as the compiler language of choice.

Pascal, named in honor of the French mathematician, is one of the most recent high-level languages developed for microprocessor systems. Pascal is a carefully structured language designed both for systems programming and applications programming. The structured nature of the Pascal language is designed to facilitate both program development and maintenance.

SUMMARY

Without doubt, assembly language is the most common language used in writing programs for microprocessor systems. Assemblers with features such as macro assembly, conditional assembly, and relocatable object code can greatly facilitate assembly language program development.

Use of high-level languages can, in many cases, greatly reduce program development time as compared with the use of assembly language. Usually, this is at the expense of memory space required for the program, and speed of execution of the program.

Both compilers and interpreters are available as high-level language translators on microprocessor systems. The most common interpretive language is Basic. The most common compiler languages are PL/M, Fortran, Cobol, and Pascal.

EXERCISES

7-1   Using the Z80 mnemonic instructions of Fig. 6-2, write an assembly language program that inputs a binary number from input port FF and displays this number as a two-digit BCD number at output port FF. The low-order BCD digit should be in data bits D0 to D3 and the high-order BCD digit in data bits D4 to D7. Assume that the binary number is never larger than 99 (decimal). At a 500 ns cycle time (2-MHz clock), how much processor time is required to perform this binary to BCD conversion?

7-2 Write the program of Exercise 7-1 as a macro where the address of the input port and the address of the output port are transferred as parameters in the macro call.

7-3 The following program is ORGed at location 0000H in memory space but execution is begun at location 0002H. The purpose of the program is to fill all 64K of memory space with zeroes. How much time is required to do this assuming a 250-ns cycle time?

```
PUSH    HL
LD      PC,HL
LD      HL,0000H
LD      SP,HL
LD      PC,HL
```

7-4 Describe the function of the following pseudo ops:

a. ORG   b. EQU   c. MACRO   d. MEND   e. IF
f. ENDIF

7-5 Write an assembly language macro that takes the sum of the A, B, and C registers and puts the total in the HL register pair.

7-6 Write an assembly language macro that will rotate the contents of any register (A, B, C, D, E, H, or L) any number of positions (0 through 7) to the right or left (R or L). Three parameters are transferred to the macro to specify each of these three items.

7-7 Write an assembly language program that will cause the LSB of output port FF to toggle between a logic 1 and a logic 0 state at a 1-Hz rate. Assume a 250-ns cycle time.

7-8 Describe the distinction between a compiler and an interpreter.

7-9 Describe the distinction between a macro and a subroutine.

7-10 What high-level language is most commonly used in business system programming?

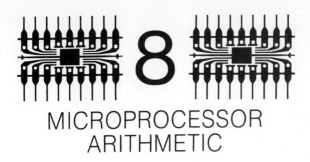

MICROPROCESSOR
ARITHMETIC

In microprocessor systems, it is often necessary to perform arithmetic operations on data. Addition, subtraction, multiplication, and division are all operations that can easily be performed in microprocessor systems. Interestingly, arithmetic operations may be done in *software* during the course of the microprocessor program or in *external hardware* that can be accessed by the microprocessor, usually through I/O ports. In this chapter, several different techniques for performing arithmetic operations in micro-processor systems are discussed.

In performing arithmetic operations with a microprocessor, straight binary notation is most commonly used for strictly positive numbers. Twos complement notation is most common when both positive and negative numbers are needed. BCD and ASCII notation, on the other hand, are more commonly used whenever data is transferred to and from external devices, such as keyboards and CRT displays. (See Chap. 6 for a description of these notation systems.)

When carrying out arithmetic operations in software, a program is required to process the operands in such a way as to produce the desired result. You will see how programs can be constructed to perform the fundamental arithmetic operations of addition, subtraction, multiplication, and division.

ADDITION

The addition of binary numbers is a straightforward operation that can be done directly by all microprocessors. A simple add instruction is all that is required. If an 8-bit microprocessor is used to add 8-bit words, and if the sum is greater than 8 bits, the carry flag (in the internal microprocessor flag register) is *set* to a 1. If the sum of the addition is less than 8 bits, the carry flag is *reset* to a 0. Many 8-bit microprocessors are also able to add 16-bit numbers (stored in double registers) by use of the double add instruction.

Example

A Z80 microprocessor is used to find the sum of 129 and 131. The number 129 is in the accumulator, and the number 131 is in the B register. The single-byte instruction required to perform the operation is ADD B; op code 80H. The sum is stored in the accumulator (replacing the number 129). The addition proceeds as follows:

$$
\begin{array}{llr}
        & 1\,0\,0\,0\,0\,0\,0\,1 & 129 \\
        & 1\,0\,0\,0\,0\,0\,1\,1 & 131 \\
        & \overline{} & \overline{} \\
\text{CY 1)} & 0\,0\,0\,0\,0\,1\,0\,0 & 260
\end{array}
$$

Since the result of this sum is larger than 255 (the largest 8-bit binary number), the carry flag (CY) is set to one, and the remainder is stored in the accumulator.

When adding BCD numbers, a special decimal adjust accumulator or DAA instruction is available in the repertoire of many microprocessors to facilitate this addition. Two BCD numbers can be added using a regular add instruction, and the result corrected to BCD notation using the DAA instruction.

The algorithm used by the DAA instruction is as follows: If the four low-order bits of the accumulator represent a binary number greater than nine, *or* if there was a carry bit from bit D3 to D4 in the previous addition, *then* six is added to these four low-order bits. If the four high-order bits of the accumulator represent a binary number greater than nine, *or* if the carry bit is high, *then* six is added to the four high-order bits of the accumulator.

Example

To see how the DAA instruction works, consider the addition of 33 and 48, both written in BCD notation:

$$
\begin{array}{lr}
0\,0\,1\,1\,0\,0\,1\,1 & 33 \\
0\,1\,0\,0\,1\,0\,0\,0 & 48 \\
\hline
0\,1\,1\,1\,1\,0\,1\,1 &
\end{array}
$$

A straight binary addition gives the result shown. To convert the result to a BCD number, the DAA instruction must be executed. Since the four low-order bits of the result represent a number greater than nine, execution of the DAA instruction causes six to be added to the result:

```
  0 1 1 1 1 0 1 1
+ 0 0 0 0 0 1 1 0    DAA
  ─────────────
  1 0 0 0 0 0 0 1
```

The number in the accumulator following execution of DAA is indeed the BCD representation of the result of the addition of 33 and 48, namely 81.

SUBTRACTION

Subtraction in a microprocessor is carried out by adding the twos complement of the subtrahend to the minuend.

Example

To subtract 11 from 16, just add −11 to 16.

```
       0 0 0 1 0 0 0 0      16
     + 1 1 1 1 0 1 0 1     −11
       ─────────────
CY 1)  0 0 0 0 0 1 0 1       5
```

Note that the carry as a result of this addition is used to *reset* the carry flag of the microprocessor when the subtract instruction is executed.

Some microprocessors have a DAA instruction that is able to correct the result of a BCD subtraction to a proper BCD number. The Z80 microprocessor, for example, has a special bit in the flag register dedicated to signalling whether the last arithmetic operation was an add or subtract. The algorithm performed by the DAA instruction is appropriately modified depending on the state of this flag bit.

MULTIPLICATION

There are two common approaches to software multiplication of numbers. The first approach is called *repetitive addition*; the second is called *register shifting*.

Suppose you wish to multiply the number N by the number M to calculate the product P. Using repetitive addition, this could be accomplished by

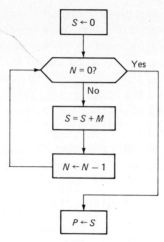

FIGURE 8-1.
Flowchart of a multiplication program using a repetitive addition algorithm. N is the multiplier; M, the multiplicand; S, the subtotal; and P, the product.

adding M to itself, adding M to this subtotal, adding M to the new subtotal, and so on for N iterations. In other words, you could write a program loop as shown in Fig. 8-1. While the method of repetitive addition is easy to implement in software, it is unnecessarily slow. Notice that if N is a number with L bits, it may be necessary to perform as many as $2^L - 1$ additions in order to carry out a single multiplication.

A more rapid software implementation of multiplication is accomplished with register shifting. Register-shifting multiplication algorithms take advantage of the following simple mathematics. Suppose that M is a K-bit number and that N is an L-bit number. That is,

$$M = (M_{K-1} . . . M_3 M_2 M_1 M_0)_2$$

$$N = (N_{L-1} . . . N_3 N_2 N_1 N_0)_2$$

M could also be written as

$$M = M_0 2^0 + M_1 2^1 + M_2 2^2 + \cdots + M_{K-1} 2^{K-1}$$

So the product of $M \times N$ can be written as

$$M \times N = NM_0 2^0 + NM_1 2^1 + NM_2 2^2 + \cdots + NM_{K-1} 2^{K-1}$$

Looked at in this way, notice that only (K-1) additions are required to perform this multiplication. Notice also that each term of this expression is either equal to $N2^x$ or equal to zero depending on whether M_x is equal to one or to zero.

To visualize the multiplication process even more clearly, suppose you were to perform the long-hand multiplication of the 4-bit number $(M_3M_2M_1M_0)_2$ by the number $(1011)_2$. Writing this out you have

$$
\begin{array}{r}
M_3\,M_2\,M_1\,M_0 \\
\times\ 1\ \ 0\ 1\ 1 \\
\hline
M_3\,M_2\,M_1\,M_0 \\
M_3\,M_2\,M_1\,M_0 \\
0\ \ \ 0\ \ \ 0\ \ \ 0 \\
M_3\,M_2\,M_1\,M_0 \\
\hline
\end{array}
$$

multiplicand
multiplier

partial
products

The product of these two numbers can then be found by the addition of the four *partial products*. Each partial product is equal either to zero or to M times some power of two. The number M can be multiplied by a power of two by simply shifting it to the left.

Example
8 × 8 bit multiply

You are now ready to consider an example program for an 8 × 8 bit multiply.

Begin with the multiplicand in register D and the multiplier in register C. Calculate the product and store it in registers B and C with the eight most-significant bits in the B register and the eight least-significant bits in

FIGURE 8–2

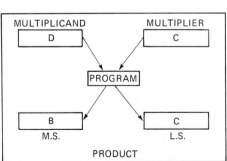

the C register, as shown in Fig. 8-2. Here is the program using Z80 mnemonics that will do the job:

```
            LD      B,0     ;INITIALIZE B REGISTER
            LD      E,9     ;INITIALIZE LOOP COUNTER (E)
BEGIN:      LD      A,C     ;PUTS LSB OF MULTIPLIER IN CY
            RRA
            LD      C,A
            DEC     E
            JP Z    END
            LD      A,B     ;B IS HIGH ORDER BYTE OF
            JP NC   SHIFT   ;INTERMEDIATE RESULT
            ADD     D       ;ADD MULTIPLICAND
SHIFT:      RRC             ;NOTE CARRY = 0 HERE
            LD      B,A
            JP      BEGIN
END:        HALT
```

It is instructive to calculate the execution time of this multiply program. Since the addition of a partial product occurs only when the multiplier is one, execution time of this program is dependent on the value of the multiplier. Maximum execution time occurs when the multiplier is equal to $(11111111)_2$ and minimum execution time occurs when the multiplier is equal to zero.

Assuming that this program is being executed by microprocessor with a clock cycle time of 250 ns, maximum and minimum program execution times can be found by simply tallying the maximum and minimum number of machine states required for program execution:

	Instruction		Number of states	
	LD	B,0	7	⎫ 14
	LD	E,9	7	⎭
BEGIN:	LD	A,C	5	⎫
	RRC		4	⎪
	LD	C,A	5	⎬ 29
	DEC	E	5	⎪
	JP	Z,END	10	⎭
	LD	A,B	5	⎫ 15
	JP	NC,SHIFT	10	⎭
	ADD	D	4	⎬ 4
SHIFT:	RRC		4	⎫
	LD	B,A	5	⎬ 19
	JP	BEGIN	10	⎭

The maximum number of states for execution is

$$14 + (67 \times 8) + 29 = 579 \text{ states}$$

The minimum number of states for execution is

$$14 + (63 \times 8) + 29 = 547 \text{ states}$$

For a 250-ns cycle time, this gives maximum and minimum execution times of

Maximum execution time = 144.75 μs
Minimum execution time = 136.75 μs

Example
8 × 16 bit multiply

An 8-bit microprocessor, of course, is not limited to performing 8-bit arithmetic. The facility with which more accurate (so-called multi-precision) arithmetic is performed is dependent on the architecture of the microprocessor and the power of its instruction set.

Sixteen-bit addition, for example, can be performed with the 8080 or Z80 using the double add instruction. The double add instruction is a 1-byte instruction that adds the contents of one of four register pairs to the contents of the HL register pair and stores the result in the HL register pair.

The double add instruction: HL ← HL + rp

0	0	r	p	1	0	0	1

r p	
0 0	BC
0 1	DE
1 0	HL
1 1	SP

An interesting special case of the double add instruction* is DAD H or ADD HL,HL which adds the HL register to itself. This doubles the value of the HL register which effectively *shifts* the HL register left by one bit. The MSB of H is shifted into CY and the LSB of L becomes a zero. You will shortly see how this 1-byte instruction can effectively perform a 16-bit shift.

---

*As an aside, it is interesting to note that the double add instruction is unusual in that during the T3 state of the M2 and M3 machine cycles, no data transfer occurs. As a consequence, the READY line of the microprocessor is not interrogated during T2.

Now consider a program that can multiply an 8-bit number by a 16-bit number to yield a 24-bit product. The 8-bit number is stored in the accumulator. The 16-bit number is stored in the DE register. The eight most-significant bits of the product are put into the accumulator, the next eight most-significant bits in the H register and the eight least-significant bits in the L register.

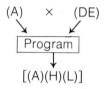

$$(A) \quad \times \quad (DE)$$

Program

$$[(A)(H)(L)]$$

Because the double add instruction will be used to aid in shifting the weighted sum of partial products to the *left* following each addition, it is necessary to begin by multiplying by the *MSB* of the multiplier. Recall that in the previous example the RRA instruction was used to perform shifts to the *right* and the program began with the *LSB* of the multiplier. You can convince yourself that these two algorithms are equivalent by writing out the long-hand multiplication of two numbers, starting first, in one case, with the LSB of the multiplier, and starting in the other case with the MSB of the multiplier.

Starting first with the LSB

$$
\begin{array}{cccc}
& M_3 & M_2 & M_1 & M_0 \\
\times & 1 & 0 & 1 & 1 \\
\hline
& M_3 & M_2 & M_1 & M_0 \\
M_3 & M_2 & M_1 & M_0 \\
0 & 0 & 0 & 0 \\
M_3 & M_2 & M_1 & M_0 \\
\hline
\end{array}
$$

Starting first with the MSB

$$
\begin{array}{cccc}
& M_3 & M_2 & M_1 & M_0 \\
\times & 1 & 0 & 1 & 1 \\
\hline
& M_3 & M_2 & M_1 & M_0 \\
& 0 & 0 & 0 & 0 \\
& M_3 & M_2 & M_1 & M_0 \\
& & M_3 & M_2 & M_1 & M_0 \\
\hline
\end{array}
$$

Now look at the program to perform the 8 × 16-bit multiply:

```
           LD    H,0           ;INITIALIZE HL
           LD    B,8           ;INITIALIZE LOOP COUNTER
BEGIN:     ADD   HL,HL         ;SHIFT HL LEFT
           RLA                 ;ROTATE MULTIPLIER BIT TO CY
           JP    NC, REPEAT
           ADD   HL,DE         ;ADDS DE TO HL IF CY
           ADC   O             ;ADDS CY TO ACCUMULATOR
REPEAT:    DEC   B
           JP    NZ,BEGIN
```

The operation of this program is shown diagrammatically below.

DIVISION

There are two approaches to the software division of two numbers with a microprocessor. One approach is by *repetitive subtraction*. The other is by *register shifting* in a manner analogous to that shown for multiplication. Having described the multiplication algorithm in detail, the formulation of a division algorithm is left as an exercise (see Exercises 8-5 and 8-6 at the end of this chapter).

SUMMARY

Microprocessor machine language instructions may be used to construct algorithms to perform the basic arithmetic operations of addition, subtraction, multiplication, and division.

EXERCISES

8-1   Write an assembly language program to perform 8 × 8-bit multiplication using a repetitive addition algorithm. Assuming a machine cycle of 250 ns, calculate the maximum and minimum times required for program execution.

8-2   Prove that the product of a K-bit number times an L-bit number is no larger than a $(K + L)$-bit number.

8-3   Calculate the minimum and maximum execution times of the 8 × 16-bit multiply described in this chapter. Assume a machine cycle time of 250 ns.

8-4 How would the algorithm performed by the DAA instruction need be changed to properly correct for a BCD *subtraction* rather than an addition?

8-5 Draw a flowchart similar to that of Fig. 8-1 but showing a division program carried out by repetitive subtraction.

8-6 Write a program to find the *quotient* of a 16-bit number divided by an 8-bit number.

8-7 What number (in hex) is in the accumulator following the execution of this sequence of instructions:

```
LD    A,37H
ADD   A,47H
DAA
```

ANALOG INTERFACES

Within a microprocessor system, all signals are represented by quantized digital values. Yet, many of the signals you may wish to input to a microprocessor system are continually-varying analog signals, such as the shaft position of a potentiometer or a voltage from a transducer. The process of converting an analog signal to a digital signal is called *analog-to-digital* or *A-to-D conversion*.

Hardware modules exist that can convert analog signals to digital format. Such modules can convert signals rapidly and accurately and require little or no software overhead in a microprocessor system. While hardware A-to-D conversion offers the capability of high-speed conversion, the required hardware is generally expensive. In fact, if conversion speed is not of utmost importance, there can be considerable cost savings in a microprocessor system by employing software instructions to aid in the A-to-D conversion process.

Two methods by which software instructions can aid in the A-to-D conversion process will be discussed. The first method employs a *timing loop*. The second method employs a *successive approximation binary search*. Following the discussion of these methods, a hardware realization of the successive approximation converter will be described. In order to understand these techniques, it is helpful to first discuss the easier task of *digital-to-analog* or *D-to-A conversion*.

DIGITAL-TO-ANALOG CONVERSION

Converting the digital output from a microprocessor output port to an analog voltage can be accomplished as shown conceptually in the block diagram of Fig. 9-1. Here, an 8-bit D-to-A converter is simply connected to the eight output bits of the 8-bit latch serving as the output port. The D-to-A

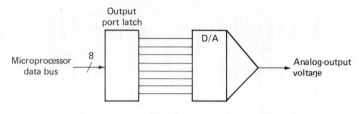

FIGURE 9–1
A digital-to-analog converter on the output port of a micro-processor is used to generate an analog output voltage.

converter is itself, at least in principle, an easy device to realize. The schematic diagram of one approach to building an 8-bit D-to-A converter is shown in Fig. 9-2. In this diagram, an *R/2R* resistor network is used to weigh, by factors of two, the relative influence of each digital input bit on the resultant output voltage. Fortunately, it is usually not necessary to build D-to-A converters from scratch. Several IC and hybrid converters are available commercially, one popular 8-bit converter being the 1408 shown in Fig. 9-3.

FIGURE 9–2
A digital-to-analog converter can be designed using an *R/2R* resistor network.

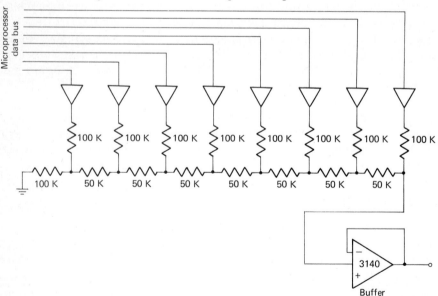

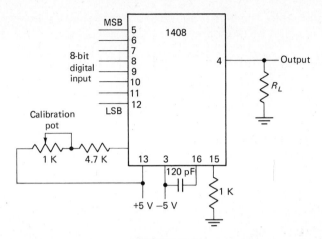

FIGURE 9–3
The 1408 IC digital-to-analog converter.

When using a D-to-A converter or *DAC* on the output port of a micro-processor, it may not be necessary to digitally latch the output port. An alternative, suitable in many applications, is to use a sample-and-hold circuit to "latch" the analog output of the DAC. As shown in Fig. 9-4, the output port strobe is used to close a CMOS analog switch (a 4066) which, in turn, allows the sampling capacitor to charge to the output voltage level. The capacitor then retains the voltage after the switch opens.

When using an analog sample-and-hold in place of a digital latch, several factors need to be taken into account. First, during the time that data is available on the data bus, the DAC itself must settle to the proper output voltage *and* the sampling capacitor must charge to within an LSB of

FIGURE 9–4
Analog sample-and-hold circuit.

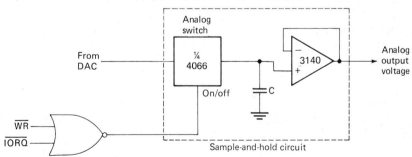

its asymptotic value. The time required to charge to this value (assuming an 8-bit DAC) is given by the formula

$$t = 5RC$$

where t is the charging time in microseconds
R is the resistance of the analog switch in ohms
C is the value of the sampling capacitor in microfarads

If data is not available on the data bus for a sufficiently long time, there are only two choices of action: (1) digitally latch the 8 bits of data, or (2) lower the microprocessor READY line until the DAC and the sample-and-hold circuits settle.

A second consideration is the retention time of the sample-and-hold amplifier. From the above discussion, it would seem that the response time of the sample-and-hold is improved as C is made smaller, and indeed it is. The smaller the value of C, however, the more quickly the capacitor will discharge. As shown in Fig. 9-5, the capacitor loses its charge through two paths: (1) leakage resistance of the capacitor, and (2) input bias current to the sample-and-hold amplifier. To keep leakage to a minimum, a capacitor with a mylar or polystyrene dielectric should be chosen. To reduce input bias current, an amplifier with MOS input transistors should be selected (e.g., a 3140 operational amplifier).

SOFTWARE TIMING CONVERSION

To illustrate an analog-to-digital conversion problem, suppose you wish to store in a microprocessor system a digital number that represents the angular displacement of the shaft of a potentiometer. The potentiometer

FIGURE 9–5
Retention time of a sample-and-hold circuit is limited by the capacitor leakage current and the amplifier input bias current.

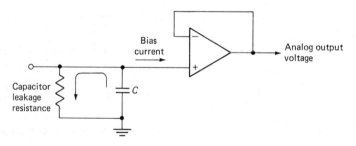

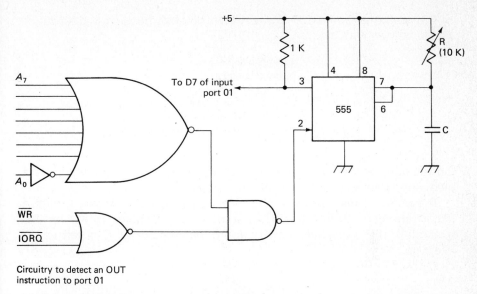

Circuitry to detect an OUT
instruction to port 01

FIGURE 9–6
Circuitry used in conjunction with a microprocessor to detect position of
potentiometer R.

might, for example, be connected to the shaft of a weather vane at a remote
location in order to monitor wind direction. The weather vane can be
interfaced to a microprocessor system using a very small amount of
external hardware and a few machine code instructions to perform the
analog-to-digital conversion.

The external hardware, shown in Fig. 9-6, consists of a monostable
multivibrator built using a 555 timer IC. The duration of the output pulse of
the monostable is dependent on the resistance of the potentiometer. For
this circuit, the pulse duration is given by the formula

$$T = 1.1RC$$
where T is the pulse duration in milliseconds
R is the potentiometer resistance in kilohms
C is the timing capacitor in microfarads

The monostable is triggered by an output instruction from the microprocessor. Following the output instruction, the microprocessor enters a timing
loop for the duration of the monostable pulse. A count of the number of
cycles through the loop is used as the digital measure of shaft position.

The software required to digitally encode shaft position in this way is shown below:

```
        LD    B,0      ;REGISTER B IS INITIALIZED
        OUT   1,A      ;OUTPUT TO PORT 1
LOOP:   INC   B        ;B IS USED AS THE LOOP COUNTER
        IN    A,1      ;THE MONOSTABLE OUTPUT IS INTERROGATED
        AND   A        ;THE SIGN BIT IS SET
        JP    M,LOOP   ;CONTINUE TO LOOP IF MONOSTABLE OUTPUT IS HIGH
        RET            ;RETURN TO MAIN PROGRAM WHEN THROUGH
```

On returning to the main program, the count in the B register will be a measure of the potentiometer shaft position.

The value of the capacitor C in Fig. 9-6 should be chosen so that a maximum count of 255 is reached when R is maximum (10 KΩ for this example). The calculation of the appropriate value for C is left as an exercise.

SOFTWARE SUCCESSIVE APPROXIMATION CONVERSION

The hardware required for D-to-A conversion is much less expensive than the hardware required for A-to-D conversion. A microprocessor executing a successive approximation algorithm can be used in conjunction with a low-cost D-to-A converter to perform the more expensive function of A-to-D conversion. The scheme for doing this is shown in Fig. 9-7.

In this successive approximation scheme, the microprocessor executes a program designed to search for the digital representation of the analog input voltage. The output of the analog comparator signifies to the microprocessor whether the current guess G_N is too high ($D_N = 0$) or too low ($D_N = 1$). Note that there must be no significant change in the analog input voltage during this search (or *conversion*) process.

FIGURE 9–7
Block diagram of hardware for successive approximation analog-to-digital converter.

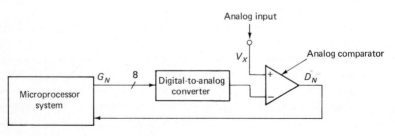

Given that all analog input voltages are equally likely, the most efficient search algorithm for the successive approximation converter is the so-called binary search. The binary search algorithm is designed so that each guess of the microprocessor yields maximum information about the value of the analog input voltage. A basic tenet of information theory is that the most information is gained when there is the most uncertainty about the outcome. With this in mind, the first guess (G_1) is the number 10000000, for it is equally likely that the analog voltage will be above or below this value. If the first guess is too low $(D_1 = 1)$, the next guess is 11000000. If the first guess is too high $(D_1 = 0)$, the next guess is 01000000. In this way, just nine such guesses are required to arrive at the answer. (Compare this to an average of 128 guesses required if you were to begin with 00000000 and simply increment by one for each successive guess.)

Mathematically, the binary search can be described as follows: let G_N be the N th guess of the microprocessor; let D_N be the output of the analog comparator immediately following the N th guess; and let V_X be the analog input voltage.

$$D_N = 0 \text{ if } G_N > V_X \quad \text{and} \quad D_N = 1 \text{ if } G_N < V_X$$

Then, the values of the guesses are:

$$G_1 = 1\ 0\ 0\ 0\ 0\ 0\ 0\ 0$$
$$G_2 = D_1\ 1\ 0\ 0\ 0\ 0\ 0\ 0$$
$$G_3 = D_1 D_2\ 1\ 0\ 0\ 0\ 0\ 0$$

$$.$$
$$.$$
$$.$$

$$G_8 = D_1 D_2 D_3 D_4 D_5 D_6 D_7\ 1$$
$$G_9 = D_1 D_2 D_3 D_4 D_5 D_6 D_7 D_8$$

The external hardware required to realize the successive approximation converter can be built from commercially available integrated circuits, as shown in the detailed schematic diagram of Fig. 9-8. Here the current output of a 1408 D-to-A converter is compared with the analog input voltage, Vin, using a LM 311 comparator. An input instruction puts the result of this comparison on the data bus.

One microprocessor particularly suited to this A-to-D conversion technique is the 8748 since it has a built-in 8-bit output port as well as a sense input T0 that can be tested by the processor. A block diagram of an 8748 system used for A-to-D conversion is shown in Fig. 9-9.

As seen in this figure, the processor sends 8 bits of data to an external D-to-A converter (DAC) on output port 1(P1). The output of the DAC is then compared to the analog input by means of an analog comparator. The

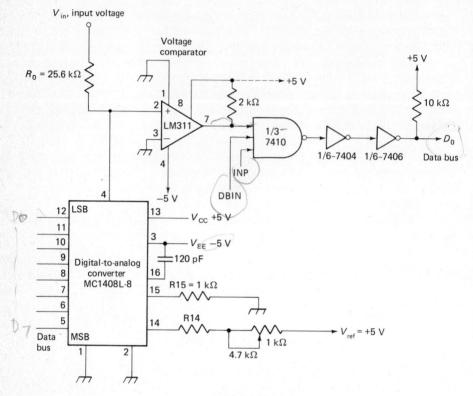

FIGURE 9–8
Digital-to-analog converter and comparator.

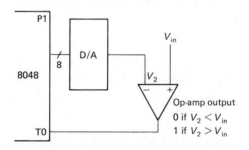

FIGURE 9–9
8748 used for A-to-D conversion.

result of the comparison is input to the microprocessor at the T0 sense input. Using the binary search technique, the microprocessor can proceed to perform the A-to-D conversion. An assembly language listing of an 8748 program that can perform this conversion is shown in Fig. 9-10.

```
            MOV     R7, #08H    ;COUNTER R7=8
            CLR     A           ;CLEAR A,R5,R6
            MOV     R5,A
            MOV     R6,A
            CLR     C           ;SET CARRY
            CPL     C

LOOP:       MOV     A,R5        ;MOVE TEST BIT RIGHT
            RRC     A           ;FROM MSB TO LSB
            MOV     R5,A
            ORL     A,R6        ;ADD IT TO PRESENT VALUE IN R6
            OUTL    P1,A
            JNTO    NOPE        ;TEST THAT NEW VALUE
                                ;IF FLAG IS HIGH NEW VALUE TOO LARGE
            MOV     R6,A        ;IF FLAG LOW, NEW VALUE RETAINED
NOPE:       DJNZ    R7,LOOP     ;GO ON TO NEXT BIT
```

FIGURE 9–10
8748 program for A-to-D conversion.

By referring to the 8748 Microcomputer User's Manual you should be able to calculate the length of time required for this 8-bit conversion (see Exercise 9-2).

HARDWARE SUCCESSIVE APPROXIMATION CONVERSION

The binary search technique of successive approximation conversion is not limited to software implementation. When high-speed A-to-D conversion is required, the binary search algorithm can be implemented in hardware external to the microprocessor. One convenient way to implement this hardware is by use of a 2502 successive approximation register (SAR). As seen in the block diagram of Fig. 9-11, the 2502, when used with an

FIGURE 9–11
The 2502 successive approximation register, used with a digital-to-analog converter and comparator, performs a successive approximation analog-to-digital conversion.

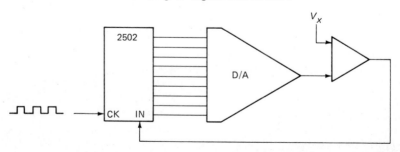

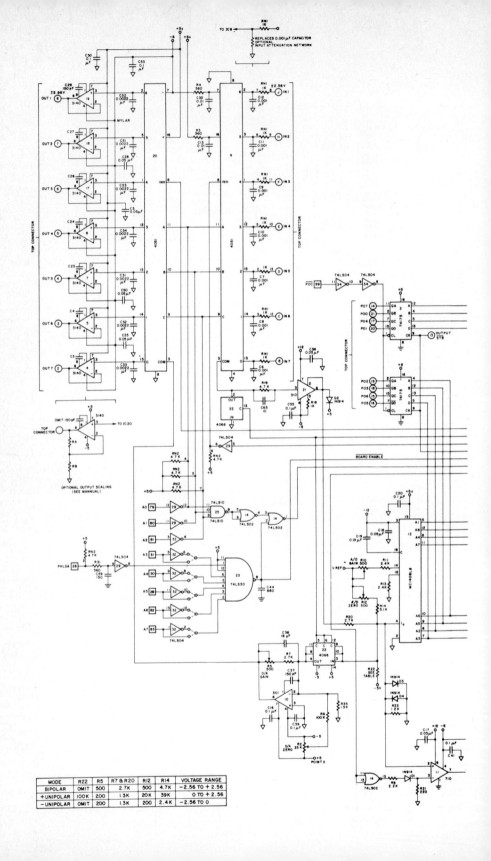

MODE	R22	R5	R7 & R20	R12	R14	VOLTAGE RANGE
BIPOLAR	OMIT	500	2.7K	500	4.7K	−2.56 TO + 2.56
+ UNIPOLAR	100 K	200	1.3K	20K	39K	0 TO + 2.56
− UNIPOLAR	OMIT	200	1.3K	200	2.4 K	−2.56 TO 0

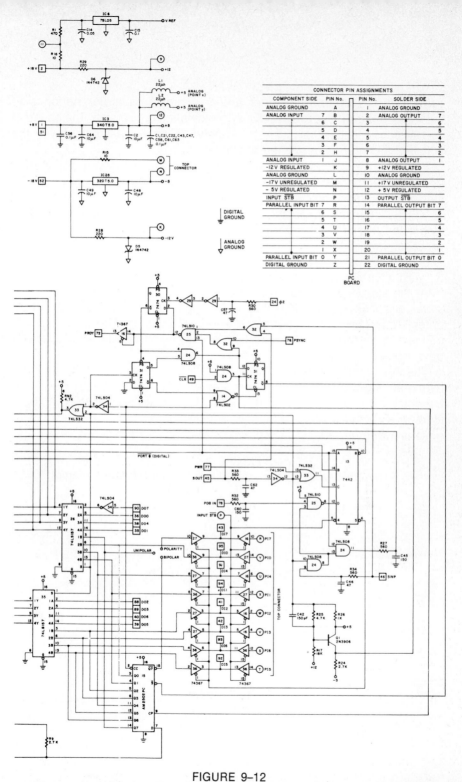

FIGURE 9–12

Multichannel analog-to-digital and digital-to-analog converter using 2502 successive approximation register, 1408 digital-to analog converter, and 710 analog comparator. (Cromemco Incorporated)

external clock, a D-to-A converter, and an analog comparator, performs all the logic required for a successful approximation conversion. The speed of conversion with this hardware is roughly 100 times faster than with the software techniques described above.

Figure 9-12 is a schematic diagram of a seven-channel A-to-D converter card that uses the 2502. The card also has seven channels of D-to-A conversion using analog sample-and-hold circuits (described earlier in this chapter). A photograph of the card is shown in Fig. 9-13. A single input instruction from the microprocessor initiates the conversion process. The READY line is then held down until conversion is complete. The total conversion time for this circuit is less than 5 μs. This card uses the S-100 microcomputer bus described in the next chapter.

At the start of an analog input cycle, the CPU sends the SYNC signal status and INPUT signal in coincidence with an analog port address. IC30 detects this event and initiates the A-to-D conversion. The SAR output is connected by the multiplexers (IC26 and IC35) to the D-to-A converter's data inputs.

The input port command for channels 1 to 7 is taken from A0 through A2 by the analog multiplexer (IC9) and is used to connect an analog input to the voltage follower (IC21). In this case, IC22 is an open circuit. Voltage follower IC21 has a very low input current requirement in combination with a fast slewing capability. This prevents loading of the signal sources and

FIGURE 9-13
Seven-channel analog interface card. (Cromemco Incorporated)

allows full accuracy for source impedances of up to 10 kΩ. Output from the voltage follower goes through R20 to inject current into the summing node at IC12, P4 and IC11, P2. After the time delay generated by IC31 to allow for settling of the input circuit, the SAR begins the conversion process.

When the conversion cycle starts, the SAR first sets its Q7 output to a logic 0 and outputs Q0 through Q6 to a logic 1. This causes the D-to-A converter to sink a current equal to 127/256 of the full-scale value of approximately 2 mA. At the end of the first clock period, the SAR checks the output of the comparator (IC11). If the analog input voltage is negative, the SAR leaves bit Q7 clear; otherwise, it is set. At the same time, the SAR also sets Q6 to a logic 0. It then waits one clock cycle before using the comparator output to set the state of Q6, and clears Q5. In a similar manner, the successive approximation procedure continues until all bits, Q0 to Q7, have been set and subsequently tested.

At the end of the conversion cycle, the SAR outputs contain the desired data word. The $\overline{CC}$ output goes to a logic 0 signalling the end of the conversion process, and allowing the CPU to proceed by outputting a logic 1 on the READY line. The CPU then inputs Q0 to Q6 and Q7 as its data. Q7 is complemented to produce a twos complement binary code, allowing straightforward bipolar operation.

SUMMARY

Analog voltages can be output from a microprocessor system by using a digital-to-analog converter to convert the digital output to an analog signal. The digital output can be latched or, alternatively, analog sample-and-hold circuitry can be used to latch the analog output of the D-to-A converter.

Analog signals may be input to a microprocessor system through various methods of analog conversion. The three methods discussed in this chapter are

1. Using software timing loops to measure the duration of a monostable pulse

2. Using software successive approximation conversion

3. Using a hardware successive approximation converter

The cost of analog-to-digital conversion in a microprocessor system can be greatly reduced by using the power of the microprocessor itself in the conversion process. If high-speed A-to-D conversion is required, though, dedicated external hardware would be the method of choice.

EXERCISES

9-1   Referring to Fig. 9-6, what value should be chosen for capacitor C such that the maximum software count of 255 is reached when R is at its maximum value of 10 KΩ? Assume a 250-ns cycle time.

9-2   Referring to the 8748 manufacturer's literature, calculate the time required to perform the 8-bit A-to-D conversion program described in the text. Assume a 6-MHz timing crystal giving a 2.5-μs minimum instruction execution time.

9-3   The on resistance of the 4066 CMOS analog switch can be as high as 280 Ω. In the circuit of Fig. 9-4, how long would the CMOS switch need to be closed to assure adequate sampling time if a 0.0022-μF sampling capacitor were used?

9-4   Given a D-to-A converter connected to output port 19H as in Fig. 9-1, write a program to generate a triangle wave at the analog output.

9-5   For the triangle wave program of Exercise 9-4, calculate the triangle wave frequency assuming a 4-MHz clock.

INTERFACE STANDARDS

As a microprocessor system is expanded by adding more memory, I/O interfaces, and peripheral devices, it becomes increasingly important that there be interface standards to facilitate the interconnection of equipment from a variety of manufacturers. Three such standards are discussed in this chapter, each with a different scope of application.

The first of these, the S-100 interface standard, provides a standard bus structure for internal use within a microprocessor system. The bus consists of 100 power supply and signal lines and is designed for signal path distances less than one meter in length.

The IEEE 488 standard is an instrument interface standard. The IEEE 488 bus consists of 16 signal lines and is designed for signal path distances less than 20 meters in length.

The RS-232 standard is most commonly used in conjunction with CRT terminals and modems. This standard is designed for the serial transmission of data over path lengths less than 15 meters in length. Newer standards, RS-422 and RS-423, are designed for the serial transmission of data over path lengths in excess of 1000 meters.

S-100 MICROCOMPUTER BUS

The S-100 microcomputer bus is designed to interface a central processor module to as many as 20 additional memory, I/O interface, or other processor modules. This bus standard was originally known as the "Altair" bus, having appeared in the MITS Altair line of computers in 1975. The bus was quickly adopted by a host of microcomputer manufacturers and was named the S-100 bus by Dr. Roger Melen of Cromemco, Inc. in August

FIGURE 10–1

The S-100 microcomputer bus consists of a bank of 100-contact connectors wired in parallel on a common mother board. The 100 lines of the bus carry address, data, and control-signal information. Several of the lines are left undefined for use in customized systems. A ground trace between the signal lines is used for shielding to reduce cross-talk and ensure reliable operations. (Cromemco Incorporated)

1976. The S-100, or Standard-100, bus is now widely regarded as "the most-used busing standard ever developed in the computer industry."*

Physically, the S-100 bus is realized as a set of 100-contact edge connectors mounted to a common "mother board" and wired in parallel, as seen in Fig. 10-1. The modules that plug into the edge connectors of the S-100 bus are circuit cards that measure 5 × 10 in, such as the Z80 CPU ("ZPU") card of Fig. 10-2. The exact physical dimensions of these circuit cards is shown in Fig. 10-3.

The S-100 bus was originally designed for use with a CPU module using the 8080 microprocessor. Although many other processors have been adapted to the S-100 bus, the bus signal definitions closely follow those of an 8080 system. The signals of the S-100 bus can be grouped in four functional categories:

---

*Dr. Rodnay Zaks in *Microprocessors—From Chips to Systems*, Sybex, 1977, p. 302.

FIGURE 10–2

This CPU card from Cromemco uses the Z80 micro-
processor. All signal decoding and buffering are
performed on the card to mate the Z80 with the
S-100 bus. CPU cards using the 8080, 6800, and
Z80 are available for the S-100 bus. (Cromemco
Incorporated)

1. Power supply
2. Address
3. Data
4. Clock and control signals

A complete listing of the S-100 signals is shown in Table 10-1.

S-100 Power Supply

Three unregulated dc power-supply voltages appear on the S-100 bus: +8
V, +18 V, and −18 V. The main power supplies are unregulated, and so
power-supply regulation must be performed on each individual circuit
card, usually by three-terminal regulator ICs.

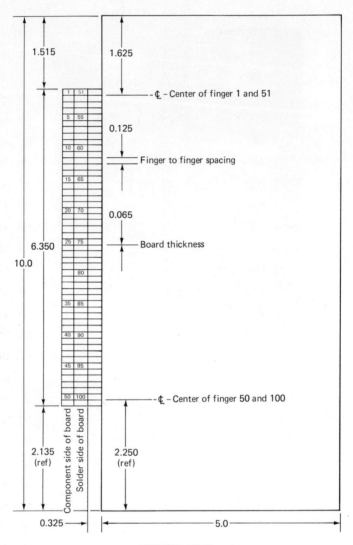

FIGURE 10–3
S-100 card physical dimensions.

Distributed power-supply regulation has several advantages over a single, centrally regulated supply:

1. Each card is individually protected from voltage overload. Faulty regulation in one master supply cannot destroy the entire computer system.

TABLE 10-1
S-100 Bus Signal Definitions

+8 V	26. pHLDA	51. +8 V	76. pSYNC
+18 V	27. pWAIT	52. −18 V	77. $\overline{\text{pWR}}$
EXT. READY	28. pINTE	53. $\overline{\text{SSW DISABLE}}$	78. pDBIN
undefined	29. A5	54. $\overline{\text{EXT CLEAR}}$	79. AØ
"	30. A4	55. undefined	80. A1
"	31. A3	56. "	81. A2
"	32. A15	57. "	82. A6
"	33. A12	58. "	83. A7
"	34. A9	59. "	84. A8
"	35. DO1	60. "	85. A13
"	36. DOØ	61. "	86. A14
$\overline{\text{NMI}}$	37. A10	62. "	87. A11
"	38. DO4	63. "	88. DO2
"	39. DO5	64. "	89. DO3
"	40. DO6	65. $\overline{\text{MREQ}}$	90. DO7
"	41. DI2	66. $\overline{\text{RFSH}}$	91. DI4
"	42. DI3	67. "	92. DI5
$\overline{\text{STATUS DISABLE}}$	43. DI7	68. MEMORY WRITE	93. DI6
$\overline{\text{C/C DISABLE}}$	44. sM1	69. $\overline{\text{PROTECT STATUS}}$	94. DI1
UNPROTECT MEMORY	45. sOUT	70. PROTECT MEMORY	95. DIØ
SINGLE STEP	46. sINP	71. RUN	96. sINTA
$\overline{\text{ADDRESS DISABLE}}$	47. sMEMR	72. pREADY	97. $\overline{\text{sWO}}$
$\overline{\text{DO DISABLE}}$	48. sHLTA	73. $\overline{\text{pINT}}$	98. sSTACK/4 MHz
Ø2 CLOCK	49. 2MHz CLOCK	74. $\overline{\text{pHOLD}}$	99. $\overline{\text{PWR-ON CLR}}$
Ø1 CLOCK	50. GROUND	75. $\overline{\text{pRESET}}$	100. GROUND

2. The heat produced by voltage regulation is thermally distributed through a larger physical volume.

3. Voltage-drops along the bus do not influence the voltage on the card circuitry itself.

4. Initial cost of the computer mainframe is lower. Regulation circuitry is purchased only as additional cards are added to the system.

S-100 Power Supply

+8 V	pins 1 and 51
+18 V	pin 2
−18 V	pin 52
Ground	pins 50 and 100

An S-100 bus mainframe capable of accepting 21 cards, such as the one of Fig. 10-4, typically has a power-supply current capacity of 30 A at +8 V and 15 A at +18 and −18 V.

S-100 Address Signals

A0	pin 79	A8	pin 84
A1	pin 80	A9	pin 34
A2	pin 81	A10	pin 37
A3	pin 31	A11	pin 87
A4	pin 30	A12	pin 33
A5	pin 29	A13	pin 85
A6	pin 82	A14	pin 86
A7	pin 83	A15	pin 32

There are 16 address lines on the S-100 bus allowing the direct addressing of 65,536 words of memory space. Tristate TTL drivers are used to drive the address bus. One control line of the S-100 bus, Address Disable, can be used to disable the address drivers to allow DMA operations when other cards need to take control of the address bus. A schematic diagram showing the address drivers and disabling circuitry is shown in Fig. 10-5.

S-100 Data Signals

DI0	pin 95	DO0	pin 36
DI1	pin 94	DO1	pin 35
DI2	pin 41	DO2	pin 88
DI3	pin 42	DO3	pin 89
DI4	pin 91	DO4	pin 38
DI5	pin 92	DO5	pin 39
DI6	pin 93	DO6	pin 40
DI7	pin 43	DO7	pin 90

FIGURE 10–4
S-100 mainframe. The basic S-100 computer can accept a number of standard 5 × 10 in cards designed for the industry-standard S-100 microcomputer bus. A large selection of CPU, memory, and interface cards offers a great deal of flexibility in system design.

FIGURE 10–5
ADDRESS DISABLE signal can be used to disable address drivers.

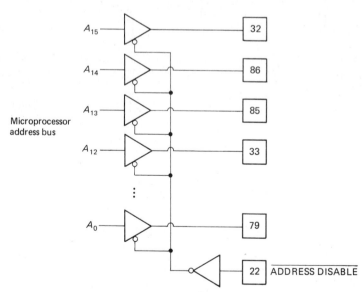

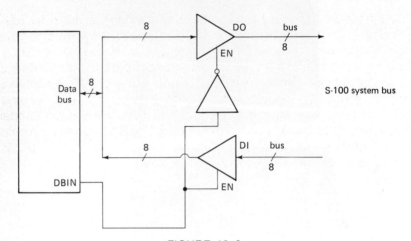

FIGURE 10–6
The bidirectional bus of the microprocessor is split into two bidirectional buses by the S-100 standard.

FIGURE 10–7
The $\overline{\text{DO DISABLE}}$ line is used to disable the data output drivers.

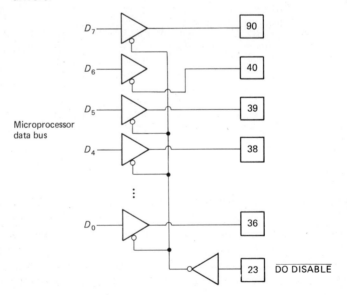

Although the S-100 bus is based on the 8080 microprocessor which has an 8-bit bidirectional data bus, the S-100 has two unidirectional data buses, each 8 bits wide. The schematic diagram of Fig. 10-6 shows how bidirectional data from a microprocessor can be split into an input data line and an output data line. In this case, the DBIN signal of the microprocessor is used to turn on the input buffer only when the bidirectional data bus is in input mode. The data input bus is called the DI bus in the S-100 standard, and the data output bus is called the DO bus. The S-100 standard provides for one control line to disable the DO bus (DO DISABLE) for DMA operations as shown in Fig. 10-7.

S-100 Clock and Control Signals

XRDY	pin 3	SSW DSBL	pin 53
NMI	pin 12	EXT CLR	pin 54
STAT DSBL	pin 18	MREQ	pin 65
C/C- DSBL	pin 19	RFSH	pin 66
UNPROTECT	pin 20	MWRITE	pin 68
SINGLE STEP	pin 21	PS	pin 69
ADDR DSBL	pin 22	PROTECT	pin 70
DO DSBL	pin 23	RUN	pin 71
Ø2	pin 24	pREADY	pin 72
Ø1	pin 25	pINT	pin 73
pHLDA	pin 26	pHOLD	pin 74
pWAIT	pin 27	pRESET	pin 75
pINTE	pin 28	pSYNC	pin 76
sM1	pin 44	pWR	pin 77
sOUT	pin 45	pDBIN	pin 78
sINP	pin 46	sINTA	pin 96
sMEMR	pin 47	sWO	pin 97
sHLTA	pin 48	4 MHz	pin 98
Ø CLOCK	pin 49	POC	pin 99

There are three clock signals on the S-100 bus: Ø1 (pin 25), Ø2 (pin 24), and Ø CLOCK (pin 49). Ø CLOCK is always a 2-MHz clock signal regardless of the processor clock frequency. Ø1 and Ø2 provide a two-phase, non-overlapping clock at the processor clock frequency. The relative phase relationships for these clock signals are shown in the oscilloscope photograph of Fig. 10-8a for a 2-MHz processor clock frequency and in Fig.

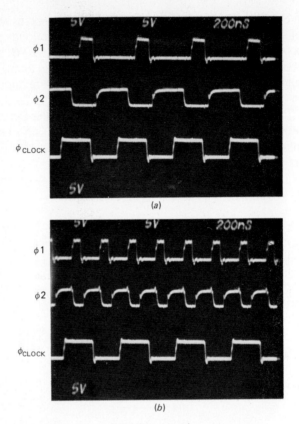

FIGURE 10–8
∅ CLOCK remains at 2 MHz independent of
the ∅1/∅2 timing. (a) 2 MHz. (b) 4 MHz.

10-8b for a 4-MHz processor clock. Notice that in each case ∅ CLOCK is a 2-MHz signal. All clock and control signals on the S-100 bus are standard TTL level.

Control signals on the S-100 bus that are functionally equivalent to control signals used with the 8080 microprocessor are prefixed with a lower case p. Thus, pHLDA, pWAIT, pINTE, pREADY, pHOLD, pINT, pRESET, pSYNC, pWR, and pDBIN serve the same function as the corresponding control signals for the 8080 microprocessor, as detailed in Chap. 3. Similarly, S-100 control signals prefixed with an s are functionally equivalent to the corresponding outputs of the 8080 status latch. These signals include sM1, sOUT, sINP, sMEMR, sHLTA, sINTA, sWO, and sSTACK. The sSTACK line (pin 98) is used to indicate stack operations in 8080 systems. In Z80-based S-100 systems, however, this line is used instead to indicate 4-MHz operation (logic 1) or 2-MHz operation (logic 0).

Four of the S-100 control lines are dedicated to tristating bus drivers (e.g., during DMA operations). $\overline{\text{ADDR DSBL}}$ is used to disable the address bus; $\overline{\text{DO DSBL}}$ is used to disable the data output bus; $\overline{\text{STAT DSBL}}$ is used to disable the status lines (those prefixed with s); $\overline{\text{C/C DSBL}}$ is used to disable the clock and control signals.

Three of the S-100 control signals shown are used only with the Z80 CPU. These are $\overline{\text{NMI}}$ (pin 12), $\overline{\text{MREQ}}$ (pin 65), and $\overline{\text{RFSH}}$ (pin 66). The functions of these signals on the S-100 bus are the same as the corresponding lines of the Z80 microprocessor discussed in Chap. 3.

The remaining 10 lines of the S-100 bus are used primarily in S-100 systems with an operator's front panel. A front-panel switch can be used to protect RAM from accidental memory write operations by issuing a PROTECT signal (pin 70) to the bus. The memory can be unprotected by the UNPROTECT signal (pin 20), and the current status of any memory (whether it is protected or not) can be determined from the $\overline{\text{PROTECT STATUS}}$ signal (pin 69). MWRITE (pin 68) is used to indicate a memory write operation and is used in conjunction with front-panel memory deposit. XRDY is an alternate to pREADY to avoid bus conflicts when both front-panel circuitry and other circuitry need control of the processor READY line.

Front-panel controls can be used to run or stop the processor or to single-step through a program as indicated on the RUN line (pin 71) and SINGLE STEP line (pin 21). When front-panel sense switches are assigned to a specific input port, $\overline{\text{SENSE SWITCH DISABLE}}$ (pin 53) is used to disable the DI bus during sense switch inputs. $\overline{\text{EXT CLEAR}}$ (pin 54) is activated by an auxiliary front-panel switch but it is assigned no specific function. Finally there is the power-on clear ($\overline{\text{POC}}$) signal that remains at logic 0 when power is first turned on and then changes to logic 1 approximately 100 ms later to indicate that power is on and power-supply voltages have stabilized.

IEEE 488 INTERFACE BUS

The IEEE 488 interface bus was developed by the Hewlett-Packard Company primarily for the interconnection of programmable bench instruments. The IEEE 488 interface was adopted as an American National Standard by the American National Standards Institute (ANSI) in 1975. The 488 bus consists of 16 lines carrying TTL-level signals. Of these 16 lines,

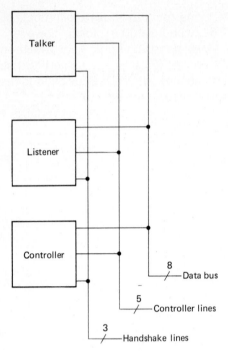

FIGURE 10–9
The three types of devices that can be
connected to the IEEE 488 bus are
talkers, listeners, and controllers.

eight are used for the parallel transmission of 8-bit data. The remaining
eight lines are used for control and handshaking operations.

As seen in Fig. 10-9 there are three types of devices that may be
connected to the 488 bus: the *talker*, the *listener*, and the *controller*. Data is
transmitted to the data bus by the talker and received by one or more
listeners. A controller is able to address specific talkers and listeners on
the bus and either enable or disable them. A controller, however, is not
required for operation of the bus. Up to 15 devices may be actively
connected to the bus at any one time.

The eight control lines of the 488 bus are grouped as a set of three
handshake lines and a set of five controller lines. The handshake lines are
used to coordinate the flow of data from talkers to listeners. The controller
lines are provided for the communication between the controller and other
devices on the bus. If the voltage on any of these control lines is less than

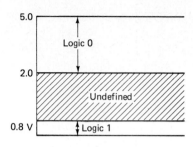

FIGURE 10–10
Logic voltage levels for IEEE 488
standard interface.

0.8 V, the signal (Fig. 10-10) is said to be a logic 1. If the voltage is greater than 2.0 V, the signal is a logic 0. Note that this convention of *negative-true logic* is just the opposite of that customarily used in microprocessor systems.

Before a talker can put new data on the 488 data bus, it must first know that all the listeners are ready for data. Once data is placed on the bus, it must hold the data there until all listeners have accepted the data. The three handshake lines are used to assure this coordination between talkers and listeners. Referring to Fig. 10-11, data transmission on the 488 bus can be seen as a four-step sequence:

FIGURE 10–11
Three-wire IEEE 488 handshake. (1) All listeners
are ready for data. (2) The talker places data on
the data bus. (3) All listeners have received the
data. (4) Talker acknowledges that all listeners
have received the data.

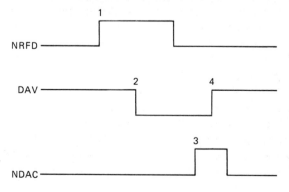

1. When all listeners are ready for data, the NRFD (not ready for data) line goes high (logic 0). All listeners on the bus are wire-ORed to this line so that if any one of the listeners is not ready the NRFD line will remain low (logic 1).

2. The DAV (data available) line is lowered to logic 1 by the talker when it places data on the 8-bit data bus.

3. The NDAC (not data accepted) line remains low until every listener has accepted the data. Again, the circuitry is wire-ORed so that NDAC cannot go high until every listener has received the data.

4. The talker acknowledges that NDAC has gone to logic 0 by raising the DAV line to logic 0.

Following this four-step sequence, NDAC goes to logic 1 once again, and the talker can then transmit the next byte of data. The data transfer rate on the 488 bus can be as high as 1 megabyte/second.

The five remaining control lines are used by the controller on the bus in the following way:

1. The ATN (attention) line is always high (logic 0) during the talker/listener data exchange described above. The controller is able to place a logic 1 signal on the ATN line to change the use of the data bus from *data mode* to *command mode*. When the data bus is in the command mode, the controller is able to use this bus to individually address talkers and listeners on the bus and either enable or disable them.

2. The IFC (interface clear) signal is issued by the controller to reset all devices connected to the bus.

3. The REN (remote enable) line can be used by the controller to disable the front-panel controls of instruments connected to the bus. This feature allows for automatic range and function selection on appropriately equipped instruments without user intervention.

4. EOI (end or identify) can serve one of two functions. In the command mode (ATN low), a logic 1 on EOI dictates that each device on the bus place one bit of status information on its specified line of the data bus. By using the EOI signal, the controller is thus able to very rapidly poll up to eight

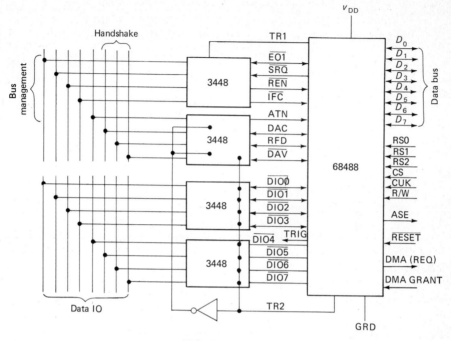

FIGURE 10–12
68488 IEEE 488 interface IC.

different devices connected to the bus. One use of this feature is in determining which of eight devices issued a service request (SRQ) signal to the controller. The other use of the EOI line is in the data mode (ATN high), where a talker can pull the line low to indicate the end of a transmission to a listener.

5. SRQ (service request) is a signal issued by a listener or a talker to the controller to request service.

When a microprocessor system is to be interfaced to an instrumentation system, the IEEE 488 bus standard can provide an effective means of doing so. A number of integrated circuits are now available to facilitate the implementation of this interface. The 68488 IC (Fig. 10-12), for example, can be used to interface the 6800 microprocessor bus to the IEEE 488 bus. As shown in Fig. 10-12, 3448 drivers are used in conjunction with the 68488 to meet the electrical specification requirements of the 488 bus.

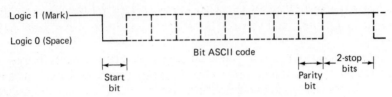

FIGURE 10–13
Serial data transmission of ASCII data.

RS-232 COMMUNICATIONS INTERFACE

The RS-232 standard (RS-232-C in the most recent revision) was originally designed as the interface standard between data terminal equipment and data communications equipment employing serial binary interchange. For example, the interface between a CRT terminal (data terminal equipment) and a modem (data communications equipment) would normally be through an RS-232 standard connection. Since CRT terminals are also commonly used as the control and display console in microprocessor systems, ¯it is only natural that the RS-232 standard would arise in microprocessor work.

Data is transmitted in serial format in the RS-232 interface as shown in Fig. 10-13. A logic 1 signal level is known as the *mark* condition and is the idle state. The beginning of data transmission is signaled by a transition to the logic 0¯state or *space* condition. One space serves as the prefix, or *start bit*, of the data transmission. Eight bits of ASCII data are then transmitted in succession starting with the least-significant bit and ending with the parity bit.* *Stop bits* of logic 1 level note the end of transmission. Normally, two

*This is the most common format in microprocessor systems, but it should be noted that the RS-232 standard does not specify ASCII data. In fact, there can be from 5 to 8 data bits plus a parity bit in the transmission.

FIGURE 10–14
RS-232 voltage levels, inverted so that a negative level represents a logic 1 and a positive level a logic 0. Signals in the transition region between +3 and −3 V are not defined.

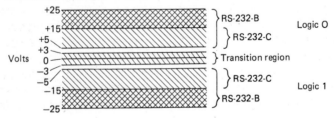

stop bits are used followed immediately by a start bit if a new character is ready to be sent or followed by a mark condition if no character is ready.

The *baud rate* of a serial data transmission is the number of bits per second being transmitted. For example, assume transmission is taking place at 110 baud. Since eleven bits are required to send each character (1 start bit, 7 data bits, 1 parity bit, and two stop bits), the character transmission rate is 110/11 or 10 characters/second.

Parallel data in a microprocessor system can be converted to serial form and vice versa by means of a UART, as discussed in Chap. 5. Separate drivers and receivers, however, are required to accommodate the RS-232 voltage and current requirements.

Like the IEEE 488 standard, *negative-true logic* is used in the RS-232 standard definition. A logic 1 level is in the range of −5 to −15 V. A logic 0 level is in the range of +5 to +15 V. (See Fig. 10-14.) RS-232 receivers must recognize signals as low as +3 V as logic 0 and as high as −3 V as logic 1. This provides a 2-V noise margin in the system. Detailed RS-232 electrical standards are given in the table of Fig. 10-15.

A number of different circuits are available for converting TTL-level signals to RS-232 levels and back again. The 1488 IC is a popular RS-232 driver, and the 1489 IC is a popular receiver. Diagrams of both these ICs are shown in Fig. 10-16. RS-232 drivers and receivers can also be realized with discrete transistors. A simple one-transistor RS-232 receiver is shown in Fig. 10-17.

A 25-pin connector (a model DB-25) is normally used as the RS-232 interface connector. Actually, for connecting a CRT terminal to a microprocessor system, only three pins of this connector need be used. Pin 2 is used for the transmitted serial data. Pin 3 is used for the received serial data. Pin 7 is the signal ground. Pin 1 is the chassis ground and may be connected to a cable shield if shielded cable is used. A list of the RS-232 connector pin definitions is given in Fig. 10-18.

In addition to the RS-232 connector pins discussed above, there are others that are used primarily with modems. Pins 4 and 5 are used for handshaking between a terminal and modem. Pin 4 (request to send) goes to logic 0 when the terminal is ready to send data. The modem responds with a logic 0 signal on pin 5 (clear to send) when it is ready for the terminal to transmit. Pin 6 (data set ready) is at logic 0 when the modem is in the data mode and at logic 1 when in the voice mode. Pin 8 (carrier detector) indicates that the modem has received a carrier tone from the modem on the other end of the line. Pin 20 (data terminal ready) indicates by a logic 0 level that data from the terminal should be transmitted by the modem. Pin 22 (ring indicator) signals a ring signal on the telephone line for use by

Driver output levels with 3 to 7-kΩ load	logic 0: +5 to +15 V logic 1: −5 to −15 V
Driver output voltage with no load	−25 to +25 V
Driver output impedance with power off	greater than 300 Ω
Output short circuit current	less than 0.5 A
Driver slew rate	less than 30 V/μs
Receiver input impedance	between 3 and 7 kΩ
Allowable receiver input voltage range	−25 to +25 V
Receiver output with open circuit input	logic 1
Receiver output with 300Ω to ground on input	logic 1
Receiver output with +3-V input	logic 0
Receiver output with −3-V input	logic 1
Maximum load capacitance	2500 pF

FIGURE 10–15
RS-232-C electrical specifications.

automatic answering equipment. Pins 15, 17, and 24 are used by high-speed modems for data synchronization.

Referring once again to the RS-232 electrical characteristics in the table of Fig. 10-15, it is interesting to note that the total load capacitance on an RS-232 signal line may not exceed 2500 pF. Since multiconductor cable exhibits a capacitance of roughly 150 pF/m, RS-232 transmission cannot be used (strictly speaking) for distances in excess of about 15 m. Partially in response to this limitation, new standards—RS-422 (for balanced transmission lines) and RS-423 (for unbalanced transmission lines)—have been adopted that can support transmission distances in excess of 1000 m. These standards will likely replace the RS-232 standard in new equipment designs where long transmission distances are important.

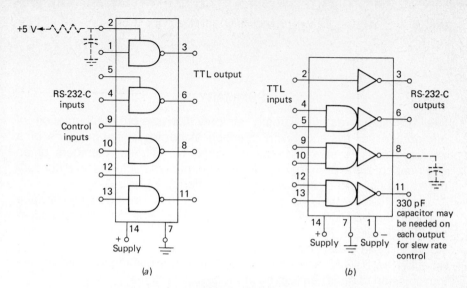

(a)

(b)

FIGURE 10–16
(a) MC1489 quad RS-232-C receiver pinout and functional diagram. The threshold levels of each receiver can be programmed by a single resistor. For noise filtering, the control input can also be bypassed to ground by a small capacitor. (b) MC1488 and RS-232-C driver pinout and functional diagram. The only external component, which may not even be needed, is a small capacitor from each output to ground to limit the slew rate.

FIGURE 10–17
Single-transistor RS-232-C receiver. The transistor and diode are not critical; most other silicon types can be substituted. For a faster rise time or more drive capability, lower the value of R2.

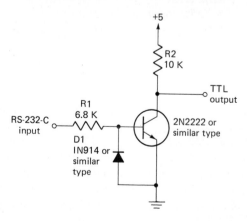

SUMMARY

Interface standards can greatly simplify the custom configuration of microprocessor systems. With interface standards, different parts of a microprocessor system may be designed by different members of an engineering team, or purchased from different manufacturers, and consolidated in a finished system with minimal effort.

The S-100 interface is a microcomputer bus designed to interface memory and I/O modules on standard 5 × 10 in cards to the microprocessor CPU. The IEEE 488 standard has received widespread use in programmable test and measurement instruments. The RS-232 standard, and more recently the RS-422 and RS-423 standards, are commonly used for the transmission of serial data in microprocessor systems.

EXERCISES

10-1 Draw the schematic diagram of an output port at address FCH connected to the S-100 bus.

10-2 Draw the schematic diagram of an input port at address 01H connected to the S-100 bus.

10-3 Given ASCII data transmitted with one parity bit and two stop bits in an RS-232 interface, what is the character transmission rate at 9600 baud?

10-4 Draw the schematic diagram of a DMA request circuit for the S-100 bus. Control signals must be generated to tristate all required bus lines on receipt of the pHLDA signal.

10-5 Describe the operation of the three-wire handshake procedure used in the IEEE 488 bus interface.

10-6 Given ASCII data transmitted with one parity bit and one stop bit in an RS-232 interface, find what baud rate is required to transmit 120 characters per second.

10-7 What is the voltage range of a logic 0 signal in an RS-232C interface?

10-8 What is the voltage range of a logic 1 signal in an RS-232C interface?

10-9 What is the voltage range of a logic 0 signal in an IEEE-488 interface?

10-10 What is the voltage range of a logic 1 signal in an IEEE-488 interface?

ANSWERS TO ODD-NUMBERED PROBLEMS

Chapter 1

1-1   BB, CB, C3, AA, F0

1-3   11000011, 00111111, 11101001, 00110010, 11011011

1-5   377, 303, 132, 356, 007

1-7   4K

1-9   7FFF

1-11 EFFF

1-13 4K

1-15 40

1-17 3

Chapter 2

2-1   94 mA

2-3   2.5 MHz

2-5   High-speed applications

2-7   Low-supply voltage or low-power applications

2-9   All applications except those requiring very high-speed or very low-power performance

Chapter 3

3-1   14 bits of address are multiplexed on the data bus. At the beginning of every memory reference cycle first the low-order 8 bits and then the high-order 6 bits are output on the data bus.

3-3   SYNC

3-5 $\overline{\text{BUSRQ}}$

3-7   ALE indicates that the address is available on the data bus so that it can be externally latched.

3-9   a) PMOS
      b) NMOS
      c) NMOS
      d) NMOS
      e) NMOS
      f) NMOS

Chapter 4

4-1   .67 Amps

4-3   88

4-5   See figure:

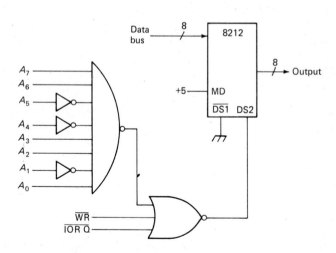

4-7   See figure following:

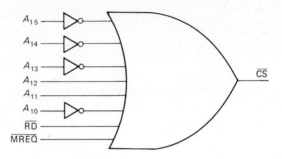

4-9 Static memories have higher power consumption and are more costly than dynamic memories. Dynamic memories require external refresh circuitry.

Chapter 5

5-1 The time delay between when a valid address is applied to the address lines and when valid data appears on the data lines.

5-3 Interrupt synchronization eliminates the software overhead of status polling.

5-5 A vectored interrupt can cause the processor to branch to any of a number of different memory locations.

5-7 See figure below.

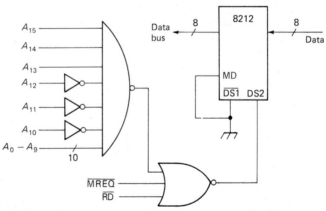

5-9 C000-CFFF

Chapter 6

6-1 a. 81
     b. 00
     c. 9A
     d. EF
     e. F1

6-3 a. 3
     b. @
     c. a
     d. 0
     e. \

6-5 41

6-7 Using the Z80, a. LD A, Address
                    b. LD A, (BC)
                    c. LD A, (IX+displacement)
                    d. JR displacement
                    e. ADD B
                    f. ADD data

6-9 00 78

Chapter 7

```
7-1           IN     A,(0FFH)
              LD     B,00H
              LD     D,0AH
        A2    SUB    D
              JP     M,A1
              INC    B
              JP     A2
        A1    ADD    D
              LD     C,A
              LD     A,B
              RLCA
              RLCA
              RLCA
              RLCA
```

```
                ADD     C
                OUT     (0FFH),A
        Minimum execution time: 40.5 μs
        Maximum execution time: 166.5 μs.
```

7-3   122.885 milliseconds

7-5   ABC-HL: MACRO
```
                LD      D,B
                LD      B,00H
                LD      H,B
                LD      L,B
                ADD     HL,BC
                LD      C,D
                ADD     HL,BC
                LD      C,A
                ADD     HL,BC
                MEND
```

7-7
```
                LD      A,01H
        A3:     OUT     (FFH),A
                LD      HL,03E8H
        A2:     LD      B,0F8H
        A1:     DEC     B
                JR      NZ,A1
                DEC     HL
                JR      NZ,A2
                XOR     A
                JR      A3
```

7-9   See text.

Chapter 8

8-1
```
                LD      HL,0000H
                LD      B,00H
        A1:     ADD     HL,BC
                DEC     D
                JR      NZ,A1
```

8-3   Minimum execution time: 81.5 μs.
      Maximum execution time: 115.5 μs.

8-5

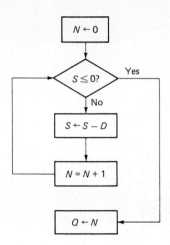

8-7   84

Chapter 9

9-1   0.17 μF

9-3   3.08 μs

Chapter 10

10-1   See figure below.

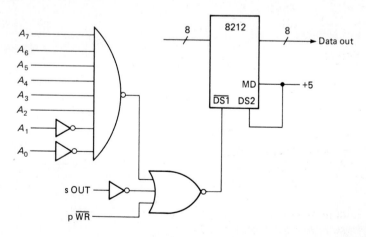

10-3   873 characters/s

10-5   See text

10-7   +5 to +15 V

10-9   +2 to +5 V

INDEX

INDEX